PUZZLES
— FROM THE —
NETHER

THIS IS A CARLTON BOOK

Published by Carlton Books Ltd
20 Mortimer Street
London W1T 3JW

A CIP catalogue for this book is available from the British Library.

Design and Illustrations: Rebecca Wright
Managing Art Editor: Andri Johannsson
Project Editor: Chris Mitchell
Puzzle Checking: Rich Cater
Production: Jessica Arvidsson

ISBN 978-1-78739-279-3

Printed in Dubai

10 9 8 7 6 5 4 3 2 1

PUZZLES
FROM THE
NETHER

A FRIGHTENINGLY ADDICTIVE PUZZLE ADVENTURE
INSPIRED BY THE WORLD OF STRANGER THINGS

JASON WARD

CARLTON
BOOKS

CONTENTS

SEASON 1

CHAPTER ONE: THE VANISHING OF WILL BYERS

CHAPTER TWO: SUBJECT #011

CHAPTER THREE: THE VOICE IN THE WALL

CHAPTER FOUR: LIFE UPSIDE DOWN

SEASON 2

CHAPTER FIVE: A ROT SETS IN

CHAPTER SIX: FEW TREATS IN HAWKINS

CHAPTER SEVEN: THE VOID

CHAPTER EIGHT: CLOSEGATE

CHAPTER 1

THE VANISHING OF WILL BYERS

WILL BEATS THE DEMOGORGON (1)
THE WHEELER'S BASEMENT

"Something's coming. Something hungry for blood. A shadow grows on the wall behind you, swallowing you in darkness. It is almost here."

Mike, Lucas, Dustin and Will are playing Dungeons & Dragons, as they do every Sunday night (unless compelled to battle a dimension-straddling predator). Mike, the Dungeon Master, thumps a serpentine figurine onto the map.

"The Demogorgon is tired of your silly human bickering. It stomps toward you. BOOM! BOOM!"

It is Will's action. To fireball the Demogorgon, he must score a number higher than Mike's as they each roll a 20-sided die. Dustin thinks Will should cast a protection spell instead: anything else would be far too risky.

WHAT'S THE PROBABILITY THAT WILL CAN ROLL A HIGHER NUMBER THAN MIKE AND THE PARTY CAN DEFEAT THE DEMOGORGON?

SOLUTION ON PAGE 156

THE BLOODSTONE PASS
THE WHEELER'S BASEMENT

In the autumn of 1983 – or the early autumn of 1983, anyway – there was nothing scarier to Mike, Will, Lucas and Dustin than the phrase "Bloodstone Pass". After playing the Dungeons & Dragons module for two whole weekends, their party had decided to head down different paths, allowing trolls to savagely kill them one by one. Their most disastrous campaign offered a valuable lesson, at least: they must stick together, no matter what.

As the first to perish, Dustin understood this fact better than the others. His executioner – a particularly sadistic troll with an unpronounceable name – cornered him by the edge of a glacier and demanded the answer to a fiendish question: "What can you put into a box that will make it lighter, yet no matter how many you put in, it remains empty?"

HOW SHOULD DUSTIN HAVE ANSWERED?

SOLUTION ON PAGE 156

ALL THE RANGE ON MAPLE STREET
THE WHEELER'S BASEMENT

Even though its exceptionally short range meant that he mostly used it to talk to Lucas next door, Mike treasured his Supercom; owning a portable device that could contact friends was astounding to him, like something from a science-fiction movie.

A few days after Mike and Lucas received their walkie-talkies for Christmas, they conducted an experiment. Mike sat in his basement as Lucas walked up and down their street, both listening until the sound dropped out. Mike's home was the fourth house away from one end of Maple Street and the ninth house away from the street's other end, and he could hear Lucas in front of every house except one.

HOW MANY HOUSES COULD MIKE THEORETICALLY CONTACT FROM HIS OWN HOME?

SOLUTION ON PAGE 156

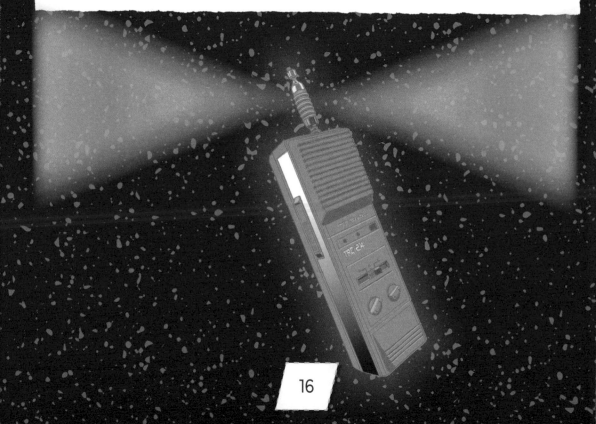

A COPY OF A COPY
THE WHEELER'S BASEMENT

Eleven had spent more time alone than with other people, but she'd learned to entertain herself. Closing her eyes, she could imagine each object in a room in its precise place, like she'd made them up out of nothing. And then she would make them float.

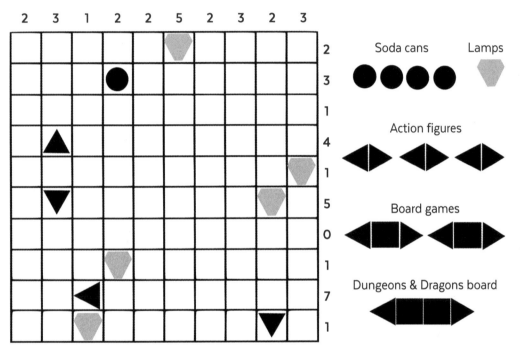

Identify the exact locations of the objects in Mike's basement. All are positioned horizontally or vertically, and none are immediately adjacent to another one, including diagonally. The row and column numbers indicate the total segments (not including lamps) in their corresponding lines.

SOLUTION ON PAGE 157

RUN! (MIRKWOOD)

His bike light flickered, and then he saw something – a shape – in the road. Will crashed, his body tumbling over the handlebars into the shadows at the edge of the wood. He was being chased. Rising to his feet, Will ran straight into the dark thickets of Mirkwood. It felt like a maze.

HELP WILL AVOID THE FRIGHTENING SHAPE AND MAKE IT HOME, WHERE HE WILL SURELY BE SAFE.

SOLUTION ON PAGE 158

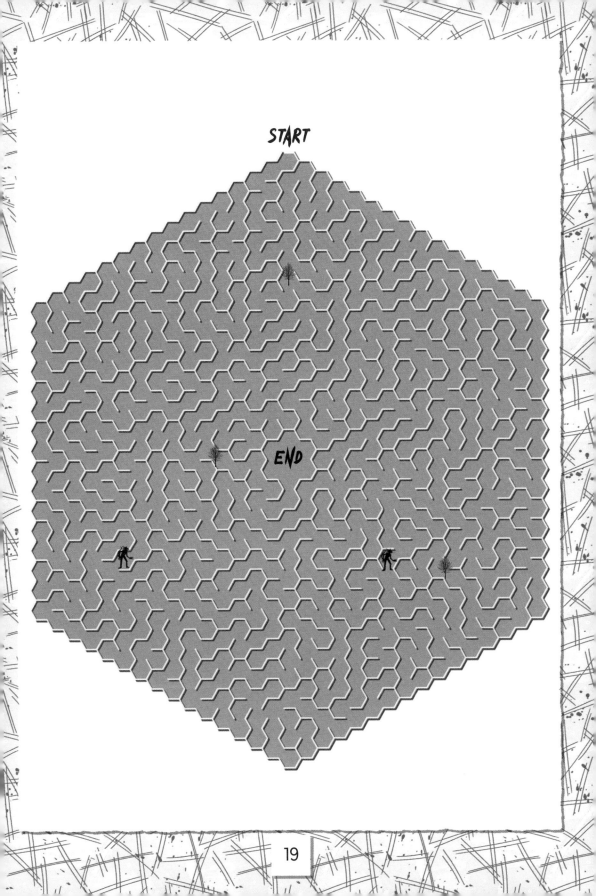

START

END

THE VANISHING (MIRKWOOD)

It had followed him through the woods and, when there were no more woods, it had followed him through his home. Now the shape had trapped him in the shed, as if this were its plan all along.

Crouched in the dark and out of options, the terrified boy tried to think of something – anything – that would distract him from the very tangible notion of his own immediate death. Will thought about a story his mother had told him that morning that she'd almost certainly made up to entertain him. In this story, she was sent home early from school one day, and decided to play in the garden until her parents returned. This was fine until she threw a ball through the kitchen window, breaking it. She couldn't recover the ball without cutting herself on the shattered glass but, when her parents came back, it had disappeared.

As Will struggled to work out the answer, something – some thing – growled behind him. It wasn't outside the shed any more.

WHAT HAPPENED TO THE BALL?

SOLUTION ON PAGE 159

OPERATION MIRKWOOD
MIRKWOOD

"Dustin, what did you get?"

"Alrighty, so we've got Nutty Bars, Bazooka, Pez, Smarties, Pringles, Nilla Wafers, an apple, a banana and trail mix." While Operation Mirkwood – also known as "Operation Getting-the-weirdo-to-show-us-where-Will-has-gone" – was only going to take a few hours, Dustin had apparently packed enough snacks to last them until 1993.

"We need energy for our travels," he shrugged.

Lucas told him that it was way too much. "Nuh-uh!" Dustin replied. "I once ate a hundred Nilla Wafers in half a minute."

"That's ridiculous. Ridiculous. On my very best day, my absolute hungriest day, after I've been in prison maybe for a decade for a crime I didn't commit, maybe I could eat half that in twice as long, tops."

"Ooh! Now that's a question. How many wafers could we both eat in fifteen seconds?"

"Why would we ever need to?"

"For stamina, Lucas. For stamina."

BY THEIR LOGIC HOW MANY WAFERS COULD DUSTIN AND LUCAS COMBINED EAT IN 15 SECONDS?

SOLUTION ON PAGE 159

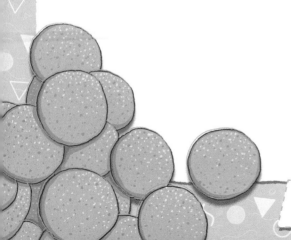

TROUBLE DOWN THE LINE
MIRKWOOD

"Do you reckon we're in danger of getting hit?" Lucas asked no-one in particular.

Dustin looked up from his compass. "By what, a train?"

"Yes."

"A train on these long-abandoned railway tracks?"

"Yes."

"Maybe?"

The pair continued endangering their lives anyway, as Mike and Eleven lagged behind.

"OK, I've got a good one. Right along the equator, two identical trains are travelling round the world in opposite directions – let's just assume that someone's bothered to build some really long bridges. Let's also assume that the trains both start together and run at the same speed on different tracks. Which train's treads will wear out first?"

"Dustin, I was there when Mr Clarke asked us that!"

"I know, but it is a good one, isn't it?"

WHAT'S THE ANSWER TO DUSTIN'S (TECHNICALLY MR CLARKE'S) QUESTION?

SOLUTION ON PAGE 159

LONG HOURS AT HAWKINS PUBLIC LIBRARY

DOWNTOWN HAWKINS

Those AV Club kids were the bane of Marissa's life. A dedication to reading is admirable, obviously, but their continued disregard for the library's sensible lending limits made a mockery of the entire institution. The four of them would arrive wanting to borrow a bunch of books on quantum mechanics or whatever it was they were into that week, and then they'd show up again a few days later wanting more books on something else and claiming it was a life-or-death situation. The fate of the world was always at stake with them!

Ten-cent fines clearly weren't working, so Marissa attempted a different approach. First, she asked the boys how many times you could take 5 from 25, but that rowdy Mr Henderson got the answer straight away. Unbowed, she tried again. She told them that she'd totted up the word counts of every single volume in Hawkins Public Library. Her efforts revealed that no two books contained the same number of words, and the total number of books was greater than the number of words in the largest book. How many words, then, did one of the books contain, and what was it about? The question completely stumped the kids: this was the highlight of her year.

WHAT WERE THE ANSWERS TO MARISSA'S QUESTIONS?

SOLUTION ON PAGE 159

It was incredibly fortunate (and long-deserved) that Donald agreed to give Joyce some of her wages in advance – her unexpected, outwardly bizarre purchases were starting to mount up. She'd already spent three quarters of the advance on replacement telephones, and then three quarters of the remaining money on boxes of Christmas lights. Now she only had six dollars left in her pocket and was sure to spend that on another couple of packets of Camels before the day was out.

The idea that she'd spent all of her money at the very place where she'd made that money was disheartening, but at least it was staying in the community, as her mother used to say, and would help her find her son inside the wall of their home, which wasn't something her mother had said even once.

HOW MUCH MONEY DID DONALD GIVE TO JOYCE AS AN ADVANCE?

SOLUTION ON PAGE 159

The owner of the Hunting & Camping Store barely looked up as the missing kid's brother and the Wheeler girl bought enough gear to capture Bigfoot. Sure, Hawkins was a quiet town, but the autumn sale was on: for a couple of weeks each year, hunting equipment flew off the shelves. Including the latest purchase by the couple (although wasn't she dating the kid with the floppy hair?), two thirds of the customers that week had bought torches, three fourths had bought gasoline and four fifths had bought bear traps. Iin fact, 26 of his customers had bought a torch, gasoline and a bear trap during that period. The funny thing was that Hawkins didn't even have any bears.

HOW MANY CUSTOMERS VISITED THE STORE THAT WEEK?

SOLUTION ON PAGE 159

Joyce wouldn't sign the death certificate. The thing they'd just shown her was not her son – she'd never been so certain about anything. How could a young boy possibly have fallen from a cliff and have his body remain so perfectly intact?

Two of the coroners – one from the county, one from the state – came down the hallway, their heads lowered with a phony solemnity that enraged Joyce. She could tell that one of the men was a liar and the other wasn't, but she wasn't sure which was which. "I need some answers about my son," she said, poking the first man in his chest. "Do you tell the truth?"

"Oh, he'll say yes," replied the second man, "but he'll be lying."

WHICH CORONER SHOULD JOYCE ASK ABOUT THE BODY?

SOLUTION ON PAGE 159

ROANE COUNTY CORONER

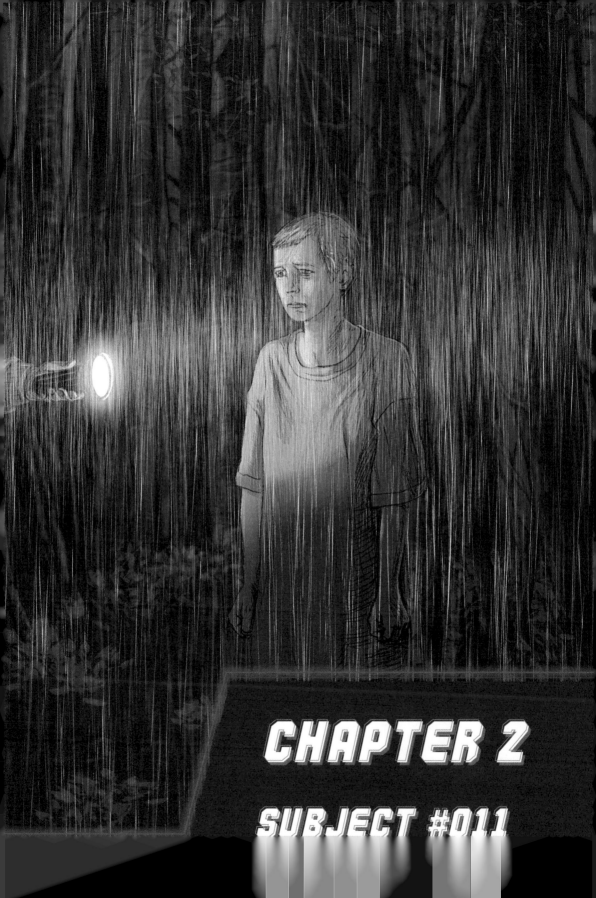

CHAPTER 2

SUBJECT #011

UNDER THE SKIN
HAWKINS NATIONAL LAB

AMULET. FRIGID. EVOLVE. AIRPLANE. APRICOT. PENINSULA.

As always, Eleven heard the words without giving them a second thought. The man in the photo would sit in another room and recite his nonsense phrases, and she would broadcast them. It was just another of Papa's tests. That is, until the day he put a different photo in front of her – a blurry one, taken from a distance – and asked her to find the man in it. "I need you to make him drink the wrong liquid," Papa said.

She could see the man, bright and shining in the void. His reflection shimmered under him in a manner that seemed familiar, as if she had seen it somewhere else before. His uniform suggested he worked in a lab, and in front of him were six bottles, a different word printed on each one: Amulet. Frigid. Evolve. Airplane. Apricot. Peninsula.

In the man's thoughts, it was clear that some of the bottles contained poisons, but not which. Eleven learned that the Amulet bottle wouldn't kill the man and that, in the pairs Peninsula and Airplane, Amulet and Evolve, and Apricot and Frigid, one of the bottles would be fatally poisonous and the other wouldn't. Also, there would be a non-fatally poisonous liquid in the pairs Peninsula and Evolve, Amulet and Frigid, and Airplane and Apricot.

WHICH OF THE BOTTLES SHOULD ELEVEN MAKE THE MAN DRINK?

SOLUTION ON PAGE 160

GRIM ARGOT
HAWKINS NATIONAL LAB

"I don't want you to hurt him," Papa said. "I just want you to listen to what he says." Eleven was unconvinced.

In the void, she saw the man. It appeared as if he was having a conversation with thin air until she walked up to him, and then it appeared as if he was having a conversation with her. The man was Russian but didn't seem to be speaking that language, or any other that she had heard before. Despite this obstacle, the code started to make its own sort of stretched logic. Eleven knew that "Yul illik har" meant "Admire good perimeters", and "Dret har camb" meant "Disarm good friends", and "Loppe yul dret" was "Quietly admire friends".

Papa was all around her now – his voice in her head, filling up her mind to its outer reaches. "Would you do something for me?" he asked. "I need you to make him say something."

HOW WOULD ELEVEN SAY "DISARM PERIMETER QUIETLY" IN THIS LANGUAGE?

SOLUTION ON PAGE 160

TATISHCHEVO
HAWKINS NATIONAL LAB

In search of some great and terrible breakthrough, Dr Brenner forced Eleven to complete task after task at the Lab, even as it sapped the life from her. Exploiting the powers that would eventually be turned against him, he made her explore rooms using her mind, starting with the one next door and venturing further and further out. He would tell her that they were just other rooms in other American labs and, for a time, she allowed herself to believe it.

Identify the exact locations of the objects in the "room". All are positioned horizontally or vertically, and none are immediately adjacent to another one, including diagonally. The row and column numbers indicate the total segments in their corresponding lines.

SOLUTION ON PAGE 160

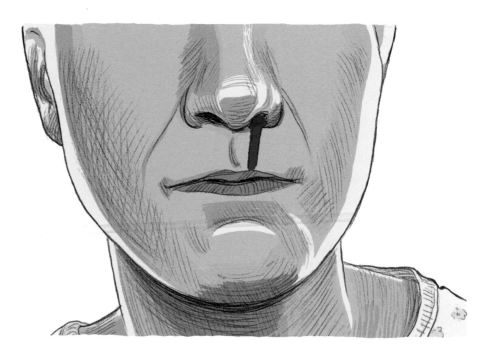

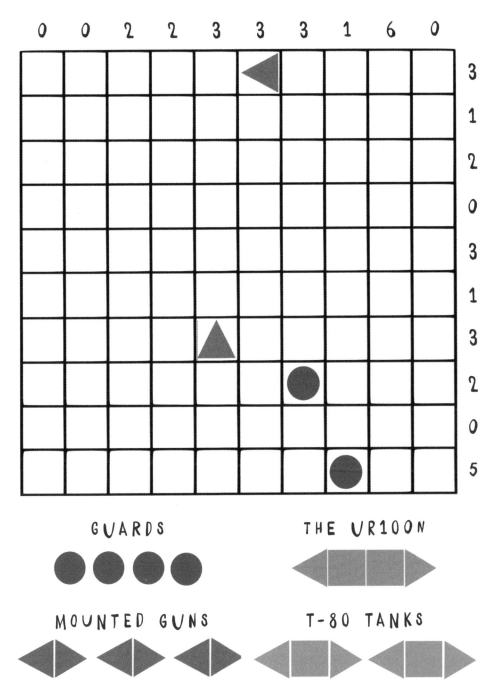

ANOTHER TIME ANOTHER PLACE
HAWKINS NATIONAL LAB

In the cabin of a fishing trawler somewhere off the coast of Montauk, a bearded man is waiting for a rendezvous, and in this man's wallet is a slip of paper, which Eleven is trying to look at.

To reveal the secret information, shade the grid's cells so that each column and row has continuous shaded blocks of the lengths indicated by the numbers at the start of that column or row, with at least one empty cell between each block.

WHERE SHOULD DR BRENNER LOOK FOR THE BEARDED MAN?

SOLUTION ON PAGE 161

		5 1 3 4 5	1 1 1 1 1 1 1 1 1	1 3 3 1 1 1 5		1 5 4 5	1 1 1 1 1 1 1	5 5 4 1 1 1		5 1 1 4 5	1 1 2	1 5 4 3 1	1	5 3 1 4 5	1 1 1 1 1 1 1 1	5 1 3 4 5	1 1	1 1 1 3	1 1 1	5
3 1 1 3 3																				
1 1 1 1 1 1																				
3 1 1 3 3																				
1 1 1 1 1 1 1																				
3 1 1 1 1 3 3																				
3 3 1 3																				
1 1 1 1 1 1																				
3 1 1 1 3																				
1 1 1 1 1 1																				
3 3 1 3																				
3 3 5 3																				
1 1 1 1 1 1 1 1																				
1 3 1 1 1 3																				
3 1 1 1 1 1 1																				
1 1 3 3 3																				
1 1 1 1 1 1 1																				
3 3 3 1 1																				
1 1 1 2 1 1																				
1 1 3 1 1 3																				

Upside Down Password
The Woods

"Ring-a-ding," said Joyce, pretending to ring the Castle Byers buzzer. "Anybody home?"

"Password?" Will asked.

"Radagast?"

"Mom, that was last week!"

Joyce squinted, her entire face scrunching up. Castle Byers, despite being mostly constructed from chestnut-oak branches, had a rigorous, ever-changing password system. "Can I have a clue?"

"Always! It's the year of this century that's the same when its number is upside down."

What's the password for Castle Byers?

SOLUTION ON PAGE 161

THE RULE OF LAW
THE WOODS

There was only one rule and it was simple: you draw first blood, you shake first. Obey or be banished from the party. This decree had proved more effort than their earlier arrangement. During an uncomfortably damp heatwave last summer, Dustin, Lucas, Will and Mike had gotten into a rare argument, with everyone at fault. To solve the matter fairly, they'd agreed that each person should shake hands with everyone smaller than them. Mike was the tallest, followed by Lucas, then Dustin and, finally, Will.

HOW MANY HANDSHAKES WERE THERE IN TOTAL?

SOLUTION ON PAGE 161

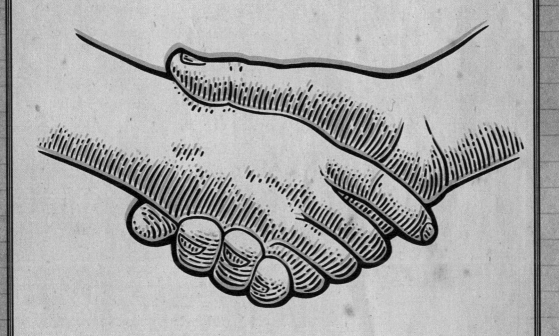

LOSING TIME
THE WOODS

With a military precision befitting both the seriousness of their mission and the style of Lucas's headband, Mike, Lucas and Duncan synchronized their watches to the correct time just before setting off into the woods. Mike, having loaned his to Eleven's wrist, was using Nancy's old watch, which ran slightly slow and lost a minute each day. Lucas was similarly challenged with his slightly-fast wristwatch that gained a minute each day, while Dustin beat them both for poor fortune with his watch that he'd broken when he tried to see if it would work underwater (it didn't).

IF THE BOYS COMPARED WATCHES AT ANY RANDOM MOMENT, WHOSE WOULD BE THE MOST AND LEAST LIKELY TO DISPLAY THE CORRECT TIME?

SOLUTION ON PAGE 162

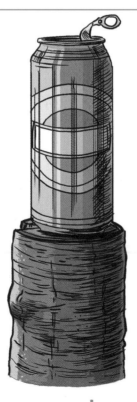

UNCONVENTIONAL GIFTS

THE WOODS

If Dustin had any talent at all – beyond science and an aptitude for memorizing lengthy chunks of the Dungeons & Dragons almanac, it goes without saying – it was that he was easily able to make people feel comfortable in his presence. This warm and invaluable quality came in use as the party followed Eleven toward the source of the electromagnetic disturbance. There was something up ther with her – she looked as if she was wearing a heavy, invisible backpack – so he posed a question:

"Hey, El, check this out: I, Dustin Henderson, have forty-five of them. Mike Wheeler has thirty-three of them, and Lucas Sinclair has thirty-nine of them. How many do you have?"

To his amazement, Eleven – who rarely spoke more than a word at a time, and had once asked "What is 'friend'?" like an alien robot who'd been rained on and then fallen down some stairs – laughed out loud and stated the correct answer.

HOW DID ELEVEN RESPOND?

SOLUTION ON PAGE 162

A Small Crime Wave
Hawkins Police Station

"Gnomes again, huh?" A deeply hungover Chief Hopper had only just made it to the station's coffee machine when his long-suffering (her words) secretary, Flo, informed him about one of the more significant crimes of the year. Some kids had evidently been stealing the gnomes out of Phil Larson's garden again. Hopper was just about to ask if someone had informed William H. Webster at the FBI when Officer Powell entered the office, trailed by three mildly embarrassed teenagers.

After several minutes of confusing cross-talk and accusations between the youths – a period during which Hopper mostly rubbed his temples and groaned softly – some facts became clear. Either Noah was innocent or Arthur was guilty, and if Arthur was guilty, John was innocent. Things got stranger: for some reason, Noah and John were adamant that they had never stolen gnomes or any other lawn ornaments together, and Noah wanted everyone to know that he'd never stolen gnomes by himself, and that, if Arthur was guilty, so was he. Hopper was so befuddled that he went into his office for a lie down.

Who stole Phil Larson's gnomes?

SOLUTION ON PAGE 162

ELEANOR GILLESPIE'S HEAD
HAWKINS POLICE STATION

Hawkins was so sleepy that it was napping lightly on the sofa. In the four long years that Jim Hopper had spent as Hawkins' Chief of Police, the worst thing to have happened was when an unidentified owl attacked Eleanor Gillespie, believing her hair to be a nest. Hopper tried to contact her to make sure that she hadn't perished from her attack, but tracking down Eleanor – even though they'd both gone to Hawkins High School together – had been something of a challenge, in part because he always got her confused with Bev Mooney and Doris... Well, he couldn't even remember Doris' surname, so no wonder. He met so many people in Hawkins – and so many of them had essentially identical hair – that all of the relevant details were tangled up in his mind. He knew that Bev, Doris and Eleanor each worked for the Hawk Theatre cinema or Hawkins Water & Sewer Authority, that Bev and Doris did the same job while Bev and Eleanor did different ones, and that, if Eleanor worked for the Water Authority, then so did Doris. What any of that meant exactly was lost to him, though.

WHERE COULD HOPPER FIND ELEANOR?

SOLUTION ON PAGE 162

SLOW CENTURY
HAWKINS POLICE STATION

Benny's exes didn't like him much, maybe, but beyond that, who would kill him? It just didn't make any sense to Earl, and he didn't mind telling Hopper as much. In the days leading up to the burger chef's mysterious death he'd been acting the same as usual – the only thing remotely out of the ordinary was that kid with the shaved head who'd tried to steal some fries from the kitchen, if you can believe that. Hawkins just wasn't the sort of town where things like this happened.

On that point, Hopper was in agreement. The last person to even go missing was in the summer of '23, at least until the recent disappearance of the Byers boy. Hawkins saw so little crime that, at the station, they'd actually started a pool to see who could arrest the most people in a year, but had to stop when the results became too embarrassing for everyone involved. At last count, however, Powell had caught more people than Callahan, Hopper had arrested more than Powell, and Callahan had a better rate of cuffing people than Simmons.

UNTIL THEY CANCELLED IT, WHO WAS WINNING THE POOL?

SOLUTION ON PAGE 162

HEAVY WEATHER
HAWKINS POLICE STATION

It was undeniable. The boss at Hawkins National Lab showed Hopper and his officers the tape of the night Will Byers disappeared, and there was nothing on it. Well, almost. "It was raining that night," Hopper observed. "Do you see any rain on that tape?"

Powell had to concede the point, but Callahan was less convinced. "Are you sure?" he asked. Hopper was. He'd spent months in front of his snowy television, the white noise calming the storm in his head. The only time he would watch anything resembling a proper broadcast was when he'd put on the weather – there was comfort to be found, he felt, in the narrow structure of a weather report. It was like a visit to an airport or an empty supermarket: no nasty developments, just the same old safe, boring place.

Lately, his banal haven had been threatened by a series of atypical weather events – who knew why, or whether they had anything to do with those power outages. Discounting the current day, Hopper knew it had rained on 13 days and, whenever it rained in the afternoon, the evening was clear, while every rainy evening was preceded by a fine afternoon. In total, there'd been 11 fine afternoons and 12 fine evenings, and he could categorically state that none of those fine evenings were the one where Will vanished. It had been raining that night, which made Dr Brenner a liar and Hopper very interested, indeed.

HOW LONG HAD THE ODD WEATHER BEEN GOING ON FOR?

SOLUTION ON PAGE 162

STRANGER QUIZZING

SEASON 1: EASY

1. Which twin brothers created Stranger Things?

2. Why does the Demogorgon attack Barb?

3. What toy does Eleven levitate in Mike's basement?

4. What has Lunchlady Phyllis been hoarding?

5. Stranded in the Upside Down, which song does Will sing to comfort himself?

6. What agency runs Hawkins National Laboratory?

7. When Hopper calls his ex-wife, Diane, what information does he learn from her?

8. What does Nancy give Jonathan for Christmas?

9. As a child, why was Jonathan once traumatized for weeks?

10. What is the first message that Will sends to Joyce through the Christmas lights?

11. Which insult does Eleven pick up from Mike?

SOLUTION ON PAGE 163

STRANGER QUIZZING
SEASON 1: HARD

1. What's the date at the very start of the first episode?

2. Which movie posters do Will, Jonathan and Mike have on their bedroom walls?

3. How big is Mike's television and how much bigger does he claim it is than Dustin's?

4. What county is Hawkins a part of?

5. What medical condition does actor Gaten Matarazzo have in real life that he shares with his character, Dustin?

6. What activity does Steve suggest doing with Nancy to take her mind off Barb's disappearance?

7. Who is Dustin excited to spot crying at Will's funeral?

8. In the hospital, what book does Hopper read to his daughter?

9. Which comic does Will request from Dustin as a prize for winning their bike race?

10. What covert CIA operation did Eleven's mother participate in?

11. After her old one is destroyed, how much does Joyce's new phone cost?

SOLUTION ON PAGE 163

CHAPTER 3
THE VOICE IN THE WALL

A COUPLE OF TALL BOYS
STEVE'S POOL

What exactly did Nancy see in Steve Harrington? Barb couldn't tell. Interested in one thing only, he'd apparently swaggered straight out of a cheap teen movie, a Bad Decision come to life and doused with hairspray. Maybe that was the appeal, she supposed, but Nancy wasn't like that, or at least she didn't used to be. Barb felt like she was losing her friend, not to a boy but to a whole other world where she didn't belong. The beers came out and Barb became uncomfortable in a vague, complicated way, as if her parents somehow knew and were disappointed in her at that very moment.

Steve and Tommy hadn't even started their beverages before they were arguing about precisely nothing: Steve claimed that he'd drunk more than a hundred beers since the summer, while Tommy said that he was boasting and that it was fewer than that. Nancy, trying to keep the peace and placate her new boyfriend for no discernible reason, said that he'd surely had at least one beer. This was all new to Barb, but not so new that she wasn't aware that only one of them could have been telling the truth. Barb sighed, looked down at the water. Nancy was going to make her chug a beer any minute now, and then there'd be trouble. She just knew it.

HOW MANY BEERS HAD STEVE DRUNK SINCE THE SUMMER?

SOLUTION ON PAGE 164

IN THE DRINK
STEVE'S POOL

Steve's party was in full swing, which, for a group of teenagers with a house to themselves for the night, meant not doing much by the pool until it was time to go back inside. During an inevitable lull in conversation, Steve and Tommy decided to play a tremendously ill-advised drinking game involving the 11 beers remaining on the table. This game, rather ingeniously, was called "Don't Be the One to Drink the Last Beer". Steve and Tommy could choose to drink one, two or three cans on their turn, and whichever competitor ended up downing the final beer would be thrown into the pool and obliged to spend the rest of the night in wet clothes ("and talking to Barb!" Tommy added, cruelly).

ON HIS FIRST TURN, HOW MANY BEERS SHOULD STEVE DRINK?

SOLUTION ON PAGE 164

LOW–LIGHT
STEVE'S POOL

Jonathan Byers is secretly taking late-night pictures of his classmates from the bushes, like a real creep. Although he will later express remorse for his actions, ultimately he will not get nearly enough criticism for this behaviour as you might hope. His photographs do help find the Demogorgon and Will, though, so that's something, perhaps.

Through his camera lens, Jonathan is looking at Nancy, who is looking at Steve. Jonathan is glum, of course, and Steve isn't.

**IS A GLUM PERSON LOOKING AT A NON-GLUM PERSON?
YES, NO, OR CAN THIS NOT BE DETERMINED?**

SOLUTION ON PAGE 164

MONSTER HUNTING
STEVE'S POOL

They'd torn the map out of the telephone directory. "This is where we know for sure it's been, right?" Jonathan said, pointing at his red Xs. "That's Steve's house, that's the woods where they found Will's bike, and that's my house. It's all so close, within a mile. Whatever this thing is, it's not travelling far."

Nancy's eyes flashed. "You want to go out there. And if we do see it, then what?"

"We kill it."

HELP JONATHAN AND NANCY FOLLOW THE MAP FROM STEVE'S HOUSE TO THE WOODS WHERE THE MONSTER MIGHT BE.

SOLUTION ON PAGE 165

START

END

THE RAINBOW SPEAKS
THE BYERS' HOME

Joyce was both distressed and euphoric: she'd been told her boy (her boy!) had died, and now here he was, glowing in the wall. She didn't know how Will was communicating but the experience was different this time. He was somehow speaking Latin, for a start, a language he'd have no reason to even understand, and his thoughts were increasingly distorted, disguised, hidden. Like there was someone listening in.

DECIPHER WILL'S FOUR MESSAGES TO JOYCE OVER THE NEXT FOUR PAGES.

SOLUTION ON PAGE 165

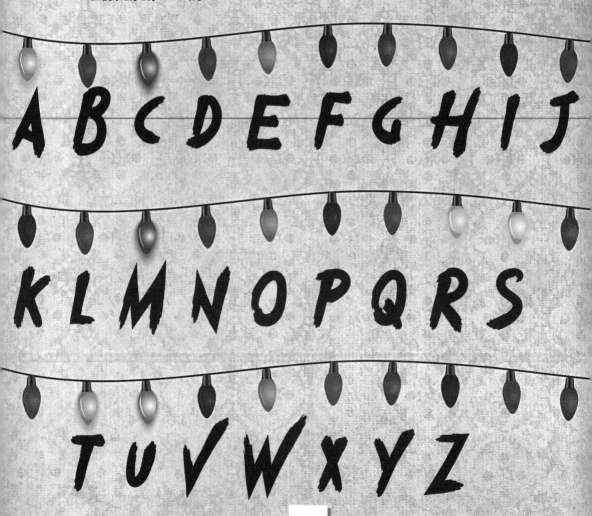

SOLUTION ON PAGE 165

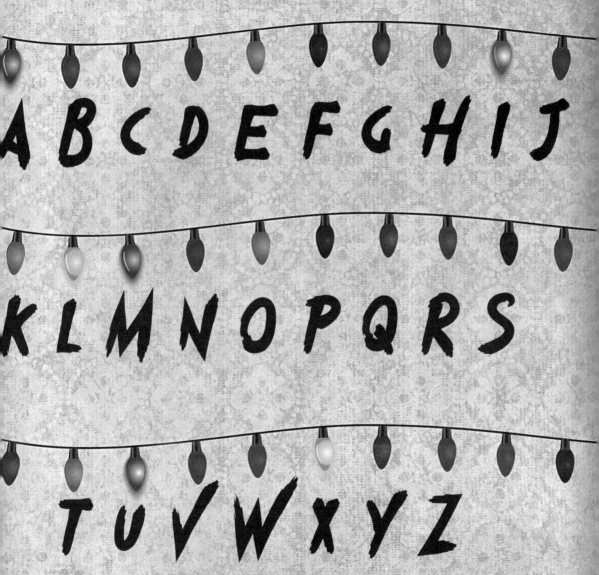

A STERN MESSAGE

THE BYERS' HOME

SOLUTION ON PAGE 166

A B C D E F G H I J

K L M N O P Q R S

T U V W X Y Z

SOLUTION ON PAGE 166

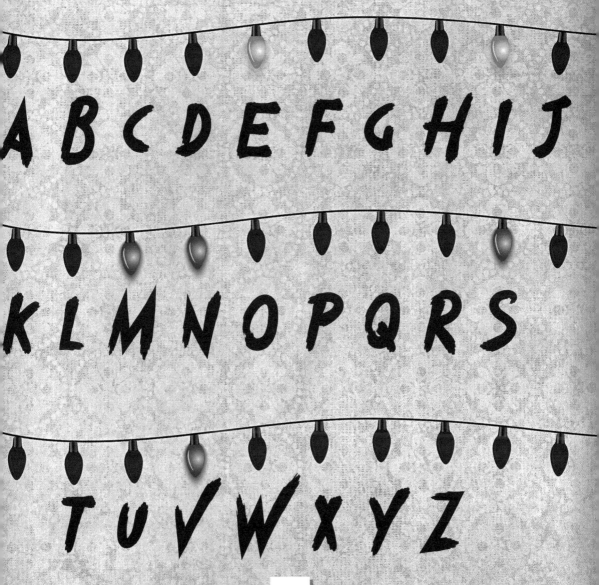

A SHORTFALL ON THE REGISTER

HAWKINS HIGH SCHOOL

Nancy couldn't actually think of an occasion when Barb hadn't made it to class before. Even that time everyone got the flu in the third grade, the two of them snuffled their way into school only to find an empty classroom and be sent home again.

The bell rang. Barb's Cabriolet wasn't in the parking lot that morning. Nancy looked over at the empty desk where her friend should be.

The teacher, such a stickler for a "well-balanced learning environment", asked everyone to move around to accommodate for Barb's absence. He didn't like teaching to empty seats, he said, so wanted six people in the front row. Nancy and five other students moved to the front of the room, but they couldn't decide which order to sit in.

HOW MANY DIFFERENT WAYS COULD THE SIX STUDENTS ARRANGE THEMSELVES?

SOLUTION ON PAGE 166

EBBING, EBBING OUT
HAWKINS HIGH SCHOOL

"The brown current ran swiftly out of the heart of darkness, bearing us down toward the sea with twice the speed of our upward progress," recited the English teacher, conspicuously reading the exact passage that contained the title of the book. Nancy was stirred momentarily from her daze. She remembered Barb's fifth-grade riddle phase – how every morning, she'd gleefully turn up with another one, which Nancy would duly have to solve. The riddles became less frequent over the years, but were briefly revived when the pair learned that the Joseph Conrad novel was on the upcoming year's syllabus:

"Heart of Darkness, Coat of Grain," Barb stated the following morning. "Was once alive, now feels no pain. Never walks but leaves a trail. Circle head and pointed tail. Grows shorter as the day goes on, its waistline is a hexagon. What am I?"

WHAT WAS THE ANSWER TO BARB'S RIDDLE?

SOLUTION ON PAGE 166

PIECING IT ALL TOGETHER
HAWKINS HIGH SCHOOL

Something terrible had happened to Barb, Nancy was certain. She studied the scraps of Jonathan's torn-up photograph: there was Barb, lonely at the pool edge, and then, what exactly? She laid the next set of scraps onto the bed. They were almost entirely blank. Turning the scraps over, she drew arrows on each piece, then brought out her Scotch tape and went to work.

To reassemble the photograph, move from top left to bottom right, stopping on each square exactly once. The arrows in each square show which direction you must move in.

SOLUTION ON PAGE 167

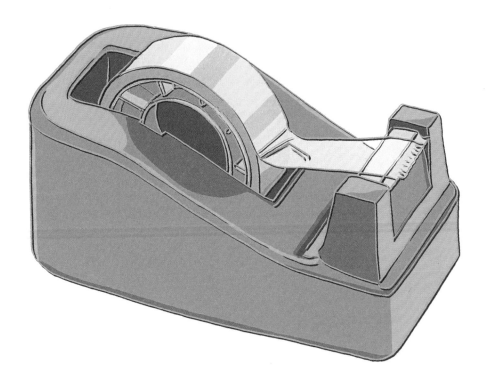

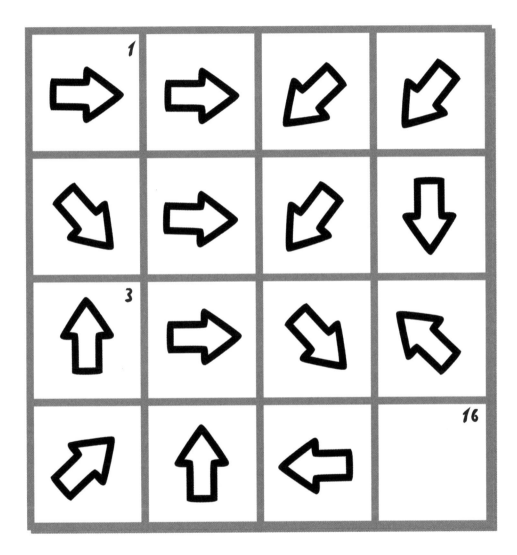

THE DARK ROOM

HAWKINS HIGH SCHOOL

Nancy and Jonathan stood in the dark room, stunned and appalled as the image materialized in front of them. It was worse than they could have imagined.

To reveal the photograph, shade the grid's cells so that each column and row has continuous shaded blocks of the lengths indicated by the numbers at the start of that column or row, with at least one empty cell between each block.

SOLUTION ON PAGE 168

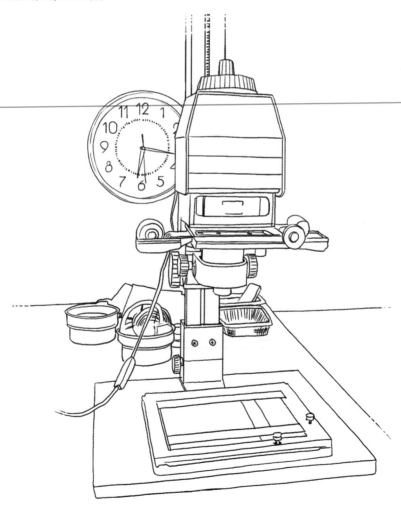

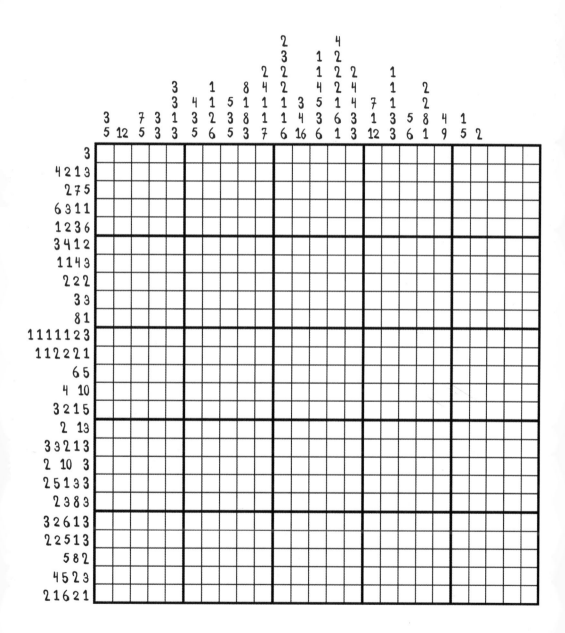

CHAPTER 4
LIFE UPSIDE DOWN

WAFFLING ON
THE EDGE OF TOWN

Until her escape, Eleven's contact with the world had been so restricted and specific that most human experiences were entirely alien to her. What was a friend? What was pudding? Eleven couldn't tell you what an umbrella did, let alone the particulars of irrigation or dentistry. Her life was a series of small rooms, occasionally punctuated by terror.

Among these many blind spots was the concept of money. For several minutes, she stood outside of Bradley's Big Buy, watching people go in with nothing and come out with armfuls of food. Just as she was wondering whether they had waffles in there, she was approached by a suspiciously merry woman. This woman told Eleven that when she entered the store she spent half of her money, and now that she was leaving, she had as many cents as she'd previously had in dollars, and half as many dollars now as she'd had previously had in cents. What Eleven had was no idea what the woman was talking about, but it didn't matter because there was a box of Eggos in the metal nest she was pushing.

HOW MUCH MONEY DID THE WOMAN HAVE INITIALLY?

SOLUTION ON PAGE 168

THE INCAPACITATING AGENT

THE EDGE OF TOWN

It was a set-up, all of it. Jim Hopper had awoken surrounded by pills and empty beer cans before, but never after breaking into a secret underground laboratory and being forcibly sedated by a man in a hazmat suit. They wanted him discredited, written off. They wanted people to think he was crazy. They wanted him to think that he was crazy.

They wanted him to stop digging.

Without a second thought, Hopper glanced at the blue ribbon on his wrist – his one comfort, his only tie to a brighter past. Tucked underneath was a thin strip of paper, scrawled in handwriting he didn't recognize:

RELi: ARTE HTFoTHGi !
LGNiLI, EGE HTNiST. IPUKO oL !

Even if Hopper wasn't coming down from a powerful government tranquillizer, he would have struggled to decode the message, but it might have made things slightly easier.

WHAT DID THE NOTE SAY?

SOLUTION ON PAGE 168

A BIT OF A LEAP

THE EDGE OF TOWN

Troy – an apparently sociopathic 14-year-old who should surely be in care – was holding Dustin at knifepoint and commanding Mike to jump off a cliff to his near-certain death. Neither Dustin nor Mike could quite believe that this was actually happening – everything at the quarry just seemed so far-fetched, which was really saying something considering that one of their friends had been recently abducted by an inter-dimensional monster and another was on the run from murderous scientists because of her psychokinetic abilities.

Dustin knew he needed to do something before Troy finished his countdown, so he tried to distract the homicidal child with a riddle:

HOW IS IT POSSIBLE TO JUMP FROM A 40-FOOT LADDER ONTO CONCRETE WITHOUT GETTING HURT?

SOLUTION ON PAGE 168

69

FLIPPING ANGRY
THE EDGE OF TOWN

Dr Brenner and his agents were closing in, but Eleven would do anything to help Mike, Lucas and Dustin - even if it involved flipping a van or two.

Help Eleven find her friends and evade capture.

Identify the exact locations of Mike, Lucas and Dustin, along with the agents and vans. All are positioned horizontally or vertically, and none are immediately adjacent to another one, including diagonally. The row and column numbers indicate the total segments in their corresponding lines.

SOLUTION ON PAGE 169

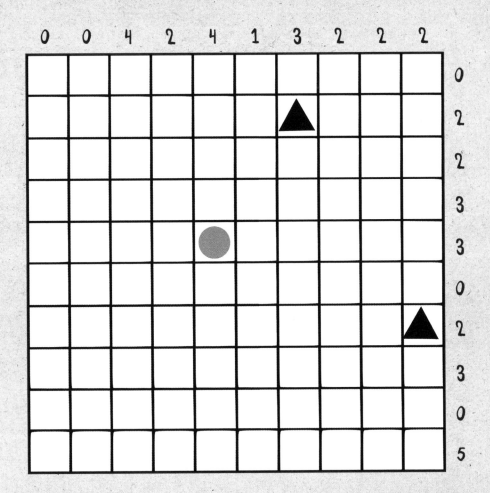

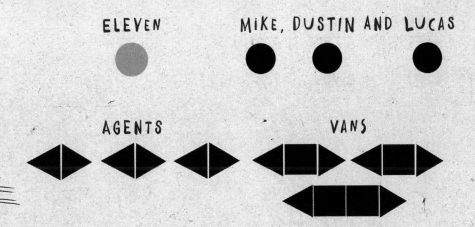

JUSTICE FOR BARB
THE UPSIDE DOWN

Barb was alone and scared and certain that death was coming. She'd woken up at the bottom of Steve Harrington's pool, but it wasn't really Steve Harrington's pool, just like this wasn't really Hawkins. It was more like a photo negative. Everything felt off, as if it worked in a slightly different way. She checked her watch and found that it was completely reversed. Despite being the exact opposite, however, it displayed the same time as when she last checked it: between 6 and 7 o'clock. All of the hours on the clock face were indicated by the same mark, and both hands were the same in length and form.

Bewildered but conscious that this was the very least of her problems, Barb climbed out of the pool. She was about to run toward home – or whatever approximated home in this place – when she spotted a boy shivering with fear. Barb recognized him from the middle school. He was a friend of Nancy's kid brother, and just as alone and scared and certain of death as she was.

In fact, the boy wasn't alone, but he didn't know it: some creature was behind him, about to attack. Barb yelled at this creature, as loud as she could, "HEY! HEY YOU!" She would never know it, but it would be the bravest thing she would ever do in her short life, as well as the last.

WHAT WAS THE TIME TO THE NEAREST SECOND?

SOLUTION ON PAGE 169

GOING SOUTH
THE UPSIDE DOWN

"Try him again," Brenner demanded, with little conviction. Although Shepard's cable had steadily lengthened throughout his absence, his radio died the moment he entered the gate, the static crackling from the lab's speakers.

"This is Shepard. Confirming, over."

A few of the men actually jumped in their seats at the development. Brenner, inevitably, was composed and inscrutable. He asked Shepard to describe what he could see.

"It's low-visibility. I'm quite a distance south of the rift. Struggled all the way! I'm only making three miles an hour. Everything's still here, but it's all eroded. Covered in blood. There's something else... There's something else in here! Pull me out! Pull me out!"

Growling. Screaming. The cable went slack. It took forever to reel it all back in, even though the winch was three times faster than Shepard's doomed trek. Finally, eight hours after the initial radio silence: the hook, the remains of the suit, the blood.

Brenner, successfully staving off guilt, wondered to himself how far Shepard had travelled, and how far away was whatever he'd found there.

HOW FAR HAD SHEPARD TRAVELLED BEFORE HE WAS KILLED?

SOLUTION ON PAGE 169

45   WILL BEATS THE DEMOGORGON (II)
THE UPSIDE DOWN

He couldn't hide forever. Castle Byers had been Will's sanctuary for so much of his life – the only place in the world that was entirely his – but sooner or later, that thing would find him and there'd be nothing he could do. He had to make a run for it while he still had a chance.

Will inched toward the entrance, every rustle and creak suddenly deafening. He could hear the thing at the treeline, its muffled wet slurps as it devoured something – what, or who, Will didn't want to think about. He took a stone in each hand and prepared to run.

Bursting out of the fort, Will hurled one stone at the beast and then the other, an awful screech telling him that he'd hit his target at least once. He hoped that it would be enough to save him.

ALL OUTCOMES BEING EQUAL, WHAT'S THE PROBABILITY THAT WILL HIT THE DEMOGORGON TWICE?

SOLUTION ON PAGE 170

VISITING THE LIBRARY
THE UPSIDE DOWN

Armed only with torches, Joyce and Hopper creeped into the Upside Down. To even be allowed this far, they'd been forced to agree never to talk about Brenner's "science experiment" with anyone, ever, but that was OK: they would find Will, no matter the cost.

After reaching a demolished Castle Byers, the pair tracked the injured monster to the public library. The building, so familiar to them since they were kids, was suddenly a labyrinth of black and pulsing tendrils.

HELP JOYCE AND HOPPER AVOID THE DEMOGORGON AND FIND WILL.

SOLUTION ON PAGE 170

START

END

A NEW ORDER
HAWKINS MIDDLE SCHOOL

The music on Jonathan's mixtapes was always excellent, but that wasn't the only reason Will loved them. Whenever he listened, he felt less alone, like his brother was right there in the room, looking out for him. Will planned to draw a picture to accompany the latest tape, but because he didn't know what any of the bands looked like, he decided to make a word search instead.

IDENTIFY ALL OF THE HIDDEN MUSICAL ACTS. SOME OF THE WORDS ARE SPELLED IN ANY DIRECTION, AND SOME DON'T EVEN TRAVEL IN A STRAIGHT LINE.

BLACKOUT

BUZZCOCKS

DAVID BOWIE

DEVO

JOSEF K

JOY DIVISION

MARINE GIRLS

REAGAN YOUTH

TALKING HEADS

TELEVISION

THE SMITHS

THE CLASH

THE FALL

THE RAINCOATS

WIRE

SOLUTION ON PAGE 171

A	D	S	A	V	O	L	N	D	I	Y	S	L	E	T
E	H	G	N	I	K	L	A	T	W	O	T	E	N	L
Z	Z	D	Q	S	Z	O	R	A	L	H	S	V	I	W
I	N	M	U	U	F	Z	E	H	E	K	F	G	S	V
T	H	P	B	R	K	N	C	C	I	N	O	I	P
A	Y	B	H	E	U	K	L	O	U	T	B	N	O	T
T	B	X	L	A	G	A	N	Y	O	V	I	S	I	K
H	E	R	A	A	S	D	H	T	U	I	D	Y	T	X
E	H	E	I	H	C	A	V	I	Y	E	J	O	H	Y
S	T	R	N	C	O	K	B	D	M	X	W	Y	E	N
M	I	I	Y	S	A	G	O	J	O	S	E	C	F	I
D	T	W	B	Z	T	D	W	U	S	U	F	M	A	R
J	H	P	I	F	S	L	I	E	T	O	K	A	L	K
O	S	Y	H	D	A	R	I	G	E	N	I	R	L	A
J	O	E	K	W	I	S	O	V	E	D	P	T	C	M

MR CLARKE ON TOUR
HAWKINS MIDDLE SCHOOL

"The Heathkit ham shack. Ain't she a beaut?" Lucas, Mike and Dustin were thrilled to see the Hawkins AV Club's newest piece of kit, but quietly, Mr Clarke was even more excited to have a receptive audience to show it off to.

"I bet you can talk to New York on this thing!" said Dustin, already fiddling. "Think bigger," Mr Clarke replied. "Imagine this: I'm at a concert in Bangor, Maine, a thousand miles away. I've brought my ham radio along and hooked it up to the instruments before taking my seat in the stalls, a hundred feet from the performers – pretty good seats! Sound, of course, travels at 1,100 feet each second, so who do you think would hear the music first?"

WHAT'S THE ANSWER TO MR CLARKE'S QUESTION?

SOLUTION ON PAGE 171

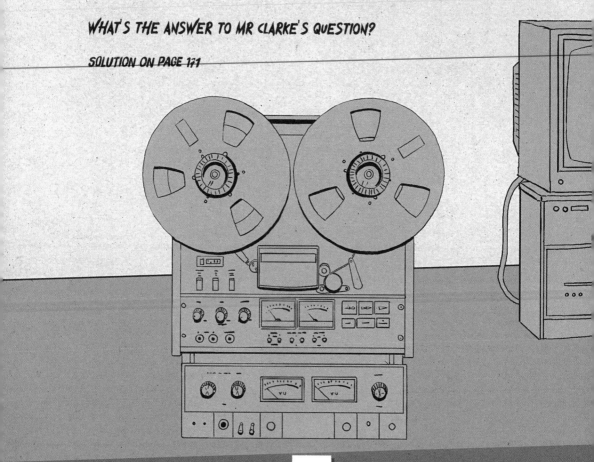

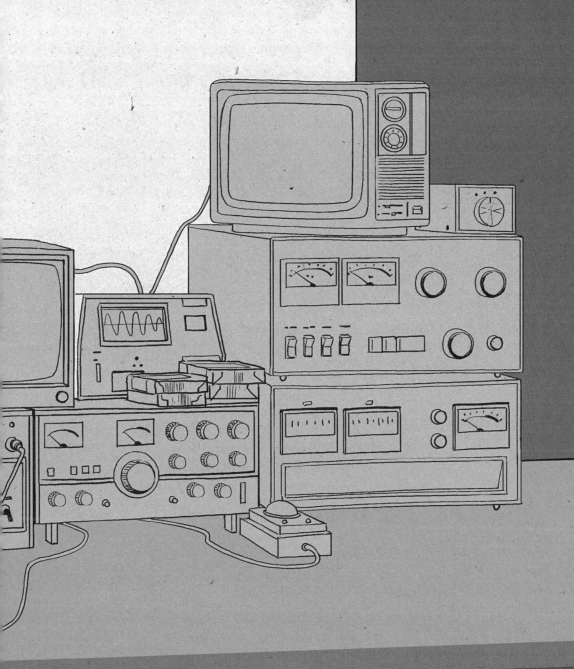

PAPER PLATES AND STRING
HAWKINS MIDDLE SCHOOL

Scott Clarke couldn't resist an opportunity to encourage the boys' interest in science. If there was anything he wanted them to take away from their time at Hawkins Middle School, it would be a desire to open any "curiosity door" they found. It was more valuable than any specific piece of knowledge he might teach them.

Fortunately, the boys were keen door-openers, which is probably why he'd ended up using a paper plate to teach them about inter-dimensional travel at their best friend's wake. Driving home that morose afternoon, Scott saw the three of them out with Mike's Swedish cousin, Eleanor. This made him think of the time he'd run into them near Bradley's Big Buy, back when Will was still alive.

They'd been on their bikes then too, and he'd given them a scenario: if he attached a string to a bicycle's bottom pedal and pulled it backward, would the bike move backward or forward? Their eyes lit up and Will ran straight inside to buy string to try it out. Scott smiled sadly at the memory: if only inter-dimensional travel really were possible.

IN WHAT DIRECTION WOULD THE BICYCLE MOVE?

SOLUTION ON PAGE 171

Eleven walked toward the pinned Demogorgon, her eyes red, blood streaming from her nose and ears. "No more," she said, and screamed the monster into ash.

She was gone.

Everything went back as it was, for a while at least. Mike was overjoyed at Will's return, although occasionally he felt that, in some fundamental way, his friend was still there in the Upside Down, that he had never left it at all. Each day, Mike would dutifully try to contact El using his walkie-talkie and, each day, he would receive no reply. Just once, though, shortly before Christmas, he could have sworn he heard something. It seemed like she'd picked a few things up from somewhere (syntax, mostly) but he would have known her voice anywhere. It was his favourite sound.

Afterward, Mike convinced himself that he'd imagined it but, for a whole day, he grinned wildly at everyone he saw. Eleven – or maybe just the voice in his head, who knew – asked him:

"A home of wood in a wooded place, but built not by hand. High above the earthen ground, it holds its pale-blue gems. What is it?"

WHAT'S THE ANSWER TO ELEVEN'S RIDDLE?

SOLUTION ON PAGE 171

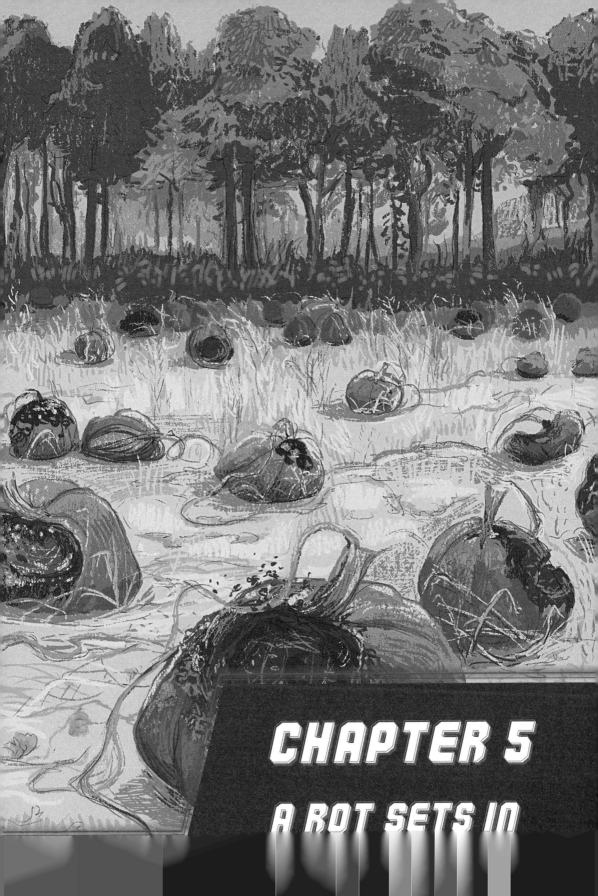

CHAPTER 5

A ROT SETS IN

Life was back to normal, or near enough. Most of the time, Hopper could almost convince himself that Hawkins was the same town he'd grown up in. Except, of course, for those nights when he'd find himself staring up at the darkness where his ceiling should be, some awful sensation in his stomach telling him that it wasn't over; that it had barely even begun.

It was the morning after one such event when Hawkins Police Department received a call from Merrill Wright, complaining about the vile actions of his pumpkin-growing rivals. He'd planted a hundred pumpkins in a square grid, only to watch with dismay as nine of them became rotten in a way he'd never seen before. This "infection", as he called it, was spreading: Merrill observed that if any pumpkin was directly adjacent to at least two other infected pumpkins, it would also become rotten.

WOULD EVERY PUMPKIN IN THE FIELD BECOME ROTTEN, AND WOULD THE SAME HAPPEN GIVEN ANY CONFIGURATION OF THE INFECTED PUMPKINS?

SOLUTION ON PAGE 172

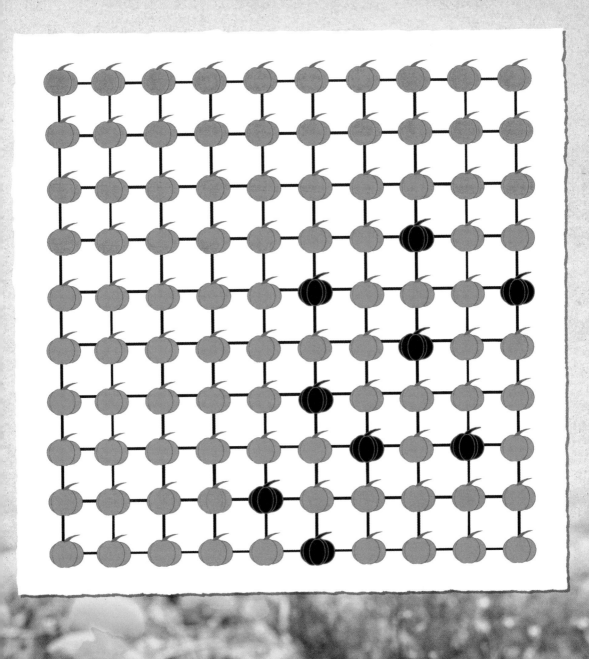

SQUASH CRIME
MERRILL'S FARM

Bad luck followed Merrill's pumpkins around. A few years earlier, Hopper was called out after an audacious robbery: always wary of thieves, Merrill had surrounded his best pumpkin patch with a 10-foot wide by 20-foot deep ditch, filled with thick mud. He considered his field well protected until the day he found his pumpkins gone and the mud undisturbed.

Relieved to have something that was technically a crime to investigate, Hopper, Powell and Callahan all rushed over to the crime scene/empty field. The trail seemed cold until Powell and Callahan each uncovered a 9½-foot plank in the nearby woods, hastily abandoned.

HOW WERE THE THIEVES ABLE TO ROB THE PUMPKIN PATCH?

SOLUTION ON PAGE 172

91

A Short-lived Heirloom
Merrill's farm

Before Merrill and Eugene McCorkle lost their pumpkins to the mysterious rot – blaming each other – each year, they had tussled for supremacy against other local pumpkin farmers (of which Hawkins had an inordinate number). For those in the know, Hawkins' annual pumpkin competition was the highlight of the town's social calendar. This said more about Hawkins' social calendar than it did about the competition, but it was always fiercely contested, regardless.

The Biggest Pumpkin prize drew the crowds, but Top Heirloom Pumpkin was for the real connoisseurs. At that year's competition, for the first time, the top prizes were awarded to six separate varieties: a Rouge Vif D'Etampes, a Jarrahdale, a Speckled Hound, a Connecticut Field Pumpkin, a Queensland Blue and a Blue Lakota. Although two of the prizes were won by one man, the farmers who won prizes were Eugene McCorkle, Merrill, Jack O'Dell, Rick Neary and Pete Freeling – the Christensens were furious about not making it in. Each variety was then entered into a final competition in which each of the six was placed, from first to sixth.

The Hawkins Post deliriously recorded all of the competition's peculiarities. For instance, the Blue Lakota and Connecticut Field Pumpkins were grown by one farmer and neither pumpkin won first or last place; the last name of the farmer who won first prize was alphabetically before everyone except the farmer who grew a Jarrahdale; neither Jack O'Dell's pumpkin nor the Blue Lakota or the Connecticut Field Pumpkin came in third; the Connecticut Field Pumpkin, the Speckled Hound and Rick Neary's Queensland Blue finished in that order, and the Rouge Vif D'Etampes received a higher prize than Jack O'Dell's pumpkin, which, in turn, did better than the Queensland Blue.

How did the farmers rank in the competition, and what pumpkin varieties did they grow?

SOLUTION ON PAGE 173

Out Standing in his Field
Merrill's farm

The outcome of the Top Heirloom competition confused everyone, but Merrill was much more satisfied with the Biggest Pumpkin contest, mostly because he won handsomely. As he and Hopper trod the pumpkin patch looking at his rotten produce a few days later, Hopper tried to congratulate him, more out of politeness than genuine interest. When Hopper asked how much the winning squash weighed – again, purely out of politeness – Merrill was tickled as he replied that the pumpkin weighed 10 pounds plus half of 10 pounds and half of its own weight besides.

How much did the pumpkin weigh?

SOLUTION ON PAGE 173

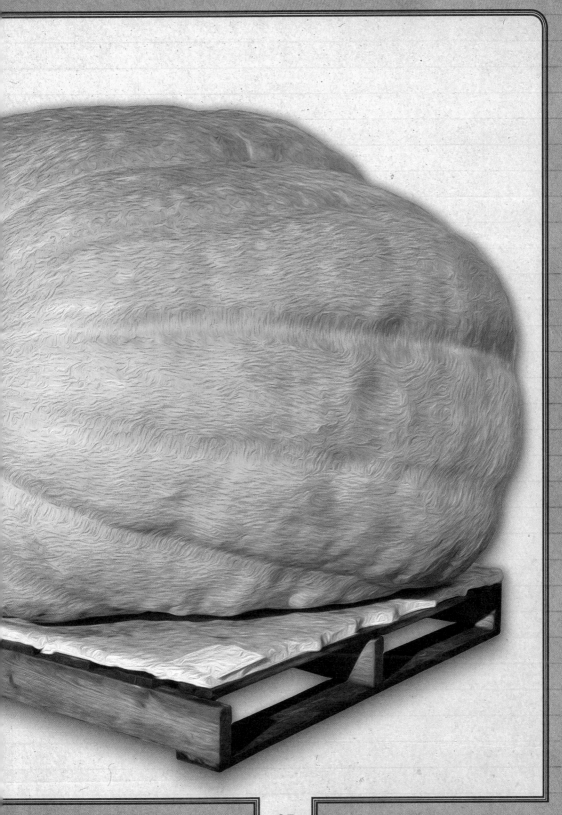

PULLING WEEDS
HAWKINS NATIONAL LAB

"I'd call it one hell of a mistake, wouldn't you?" Dr Owens gestured toward a mass of black tendrils that you could smell from the next room. He was giving Nancy and Jonathan a tour of Hawkins National Lab, hoping to dissuade them from telling Marsha Holland the truth about her daughter's death. "See, the thing is, we can't seem to erase our mistake, but we can try to stop it spreading. It's just like pulling weeds."

Behind him, a man in a hazmat suit was burning the vines. As soon as he finished, more took their place. Owens sighed. "All living organisms develop defence mechanisms against attack. We've been burning them until now, but its effectiveness is diminishing. Separating them seems to work for now though, so every single day Teddy here puts twenty-seven tendrils in four cages. He can put any number of tendrils in each cage, but the problem is that the total number in each cage must be an odd number, otherwise – you guessed it – they replicate."

HOW DOES TEDDY ACCOMPLISH THIS?

SOLUTION ON PAGE 173

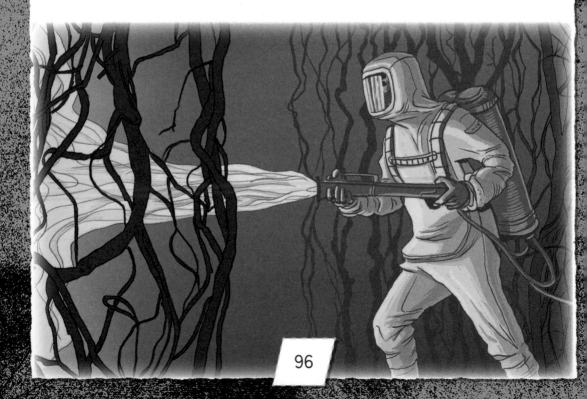

LONG NIGHT
HAWKINS NATIONAL LAB

Owens didn't even need a microscope anymore; he could see it with his own eyes: every minute, the tendrils split into two. At 22:00, he put the latest sample from what they called "the Nether" into a beaker and, at exactly 23:00, the beaker was full. As a scientist, he was trained to be calm and observant, but he felt like wailing.

AT WHAT TIME WAS THE BEAKER HALF FULL?

SOLUTION ON PAGE 173

BREEDING FRENZY
HAWKINS NATIONAL LAB

The tunnels spreading beneath Hawkins took up so much attention that it took the scientists at the lab months to notice the ash-like material floating in the air. They referred to it as "spores", but closer examination revealed them to be miniscule organisms separate from the tunnels. Their reproductive speed horrified: each female "spore" was capable of producing 120 eggs at a time, dying immediately afterward. Half of these spores would be females and would grow enough after 20 days to produce more eggs.

IF A SINGLE SPORE PRODUCED ITS FIRST EGGS ON 1 APRIL 1984, HOW MANY EGGS WOULD BE PRODUCED AT THE END OF THE SUMMER, SEVEN GENERATIONS LATER?

SOLUTION ON PAGE 173

HAWKINS NATIONAL LAB

Every time Joyce brought Will to the lab, they mostly discussed candy. Joyce understood that such small talk was a way for Dr Owens to observe how Will responded to certain stimuli but, obviously, to mention this would invalidate the tests, so she remained quiet and listened to debate after debate on the merits of nougat.

On their most recent visit, Dr Owens asked Will – life or death – to pick a desert-island candy. Like any 12-year-old asked to rate confectionery, Will treated the matter with the seriousness it deserved, concluding that his favourite was Reese's Pieces. Dr Owens, giving his rebuttal, said that he preferred Mounds bars, but conceded that peanut butter and chocolate was hard to beat. He then said something that made Will scrunch up his face:

"All kids are Mounds fans. Some Mounds fans are also Three Musketeers fans. Some Three Musketeers fans are also Reese's Pieces fans. Therefore, some kids are Reese's Pieces fans."

IF THE FIRST THREE STATEMENTS ARE TRUE, IS THE CONCLUSION TRUE OR FALSE?

SOLUTION ON PAGE 174

OLD MAN HUMPHREY
PALACE ARCADE

While Dustin looked for change under sofas and Mike committed minor larceny in his sister's bedroom, Lucas was "doing real work, like a man." This real work mostly entailed mowing Old Man Humphrey's lawn, but he figured it was still better than robbing a sibling. Also, even though she was much younger than him, Lucas wouldn't dare rob his own sister. Erica was mean.

Dustin couldn't believe that a person in 1984 could actually be referred to as "Old Man Humphrey", even ironically, but the hackneyed nickname was a perfect fit. The last time Lucas mowed his lawn, near the start of summer, OMH made a proposal: Lucas would be employed for half an hour and would be paid $8 for each minute that he worked, on the condition that that he would forfeit $10 for each minute that he idled. As Lucas mowed the lawn, he was giddy thinking about all the money he was going to take home but, at the end of the 30 minutes, Old Man Humphrey mischievously declared that neither owed the other anything.

This time, fortunately, they agreed the price in advance: Lucas had made 20 quarters, which would last him an hour on Dig Dug or about two minutes on Dragon's Lair.

HOW LONG DID OMH CLAIM LUCAS WORKED FOR AND HOW LONG DID HE IDLE?

SOLUTION ON PAGE 174

Everyone agreed that Dragon's Lair was an overpriced rip-off but, even if it cost a million quarters (Dustin's estimate) to complete, at least there was the promise of finally winning the heart of Princess Daphne at the end. What did Mr Target! offer except high-speed maths and concentric shapes? Mr Target! was the only machine at the Palace that Max, Dustin, Lucas and Mike were all steadfastly uninterested in, and yet the only game that Will was actually good at. This probably wasn't a coincidence: Will always felt most comfortable when quietly doing his own thing, without having to compete against his friends or show anyone up.

The object of Mr Target! was to get a score of 100. The problem – beyond the difficulty of even hitting the board, which seemed to elude everyone bar Will – was that each shot cost a quarter.

HOW COULD WILL BEAT THE GAME AND HOW MANY QUARTERS WOULD IT COST?

SOLUTION ON PAGE 174

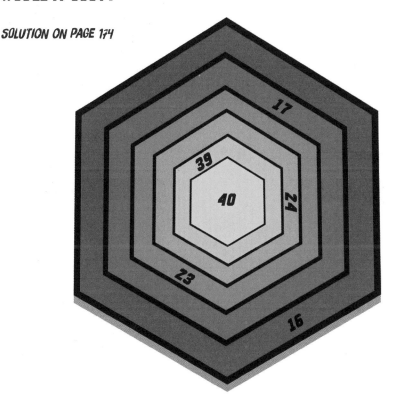

Sure, Dustin's friends had faced some personal issues lately, there was no denying that, but were any of them being haunted by a superior arcade player? It's one thing to be abducted into an alternate dimension and then possessed by a malevolent shadow monster, but had any of his pals ever had their hard-earned Centipede and Dig Dug scores toppled overnight by a gaming demon? When Keith tipped him off that the Palace was getting a new machine called Arrow-Barrow, Dustin envisaged his only hope of beating MADMAX: if he played it enough before her, maybe he could stay ahead forever. This was folly, Dustin knew, but folly was all he had.

He went by himself to the arcade, pockets bulging with quarters. Despite the exhilarating images drawn on the side of the cabinet, the game primarily involved moving a pixelated barrow from the top of the screen to the bottom, jumping from arrow to arrow.

To win the level, move from top left to bottom right, stopping on each square exactly once. The arrows in each square show which direction you must move in.

SOLUTION ON PAGE 175

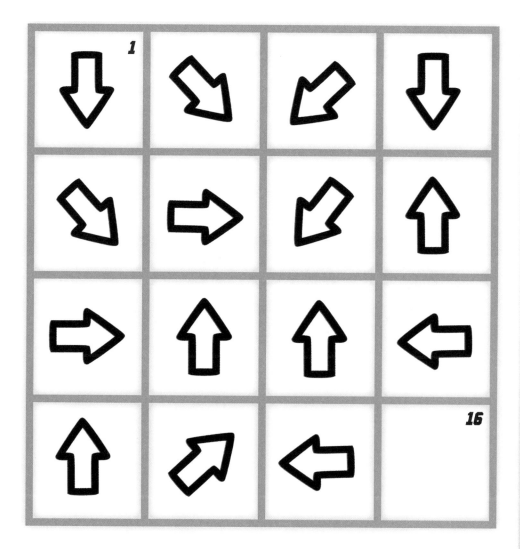

1ST 751300 MADMAX
PALACE ARCADE

If he didn't take it so hard, it wouldn't be such a pleasure to overturn Dustin's scores. Usually, Max played by herself, but the Palace – emboldened by an arcade craze that would surely never wane – had bought yet another new machine, and the chance to obliterate Dustin in person was too good to miss.

The pair took turns to see who could escape the maze fastest. Dustin went first but, although Max suspected that he'd been playing Monty Steps Out! ahead of time, he was a shambles in her presence for some reason.

HELP MAX CRUSH DUSTIN (AGAIN)

SOLUTION ON PAGE 176

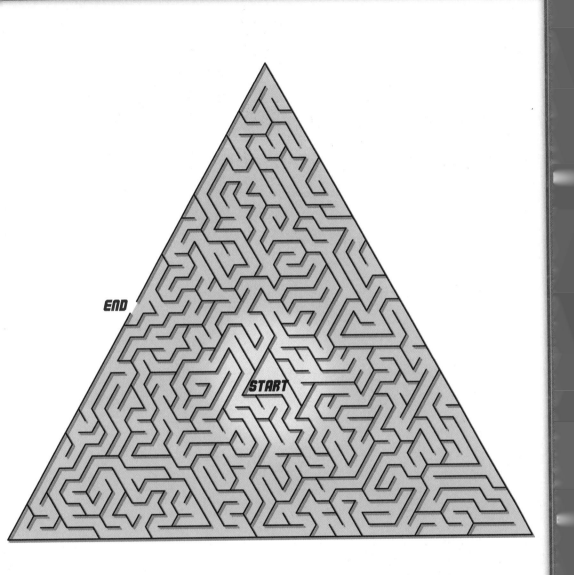

CHAPTER 6
FEW TREATS IN HAWKINS

"I call them the 'Don't Be Stupid' Rules because we're not stupid.

Rule number one: always keep the curtains drawn.

Rule number two: only open the door if you hear my secret knock.

And rule number three: don't ever go out alone, especially not in the daylight. That's it."

Hopper had only one mission in life: to make sure that nothing bad ever happened to Eleven again, even if it meant her never going outside again. Their cabin was well-protected but the chief had a nagging fear that he'd purchased the wrong number of tripwires. If he put a tripwire in front of each door, he had one tripwire too many but, if he put two tripwires in front of each door, he had one door too many.

HOW MANY DOORS DID THE CABIN HAVE, AND HOW MANY TRIPWIRES HAD HOPPER BOUGHT?

SOLUTION ON PAGE 177

A person who cannot leave the house has a lot of time on their hands. As much as Eleven wanted to spend every hour of that time watching TV, Hopper insisted upon activities that developed her abilities in critical thinking, communication, logical reasoning and solving murders in secret passage-strewn English country houses.

Hopper soon learned, however, that he was the one in need of mental development: over the course of their first four months living together, Eleven won 60 per cent of the board games they played, and was only getting better.

OVER THE REST OF THE YEAR, WHAT PERCENTAGE OF THE REMAINING GAMES MUST ELEVEN WIN TO HAVE WON 80 PER CENT OF ALL OF THE GAMES?

SOLUTION ON PAGE 177

Night School
Hopper's Cabin

Hopper was no Mr Clarke, but he certainly tried his best. He'd driven out of town to buy all of the right textbooks for a child of Eleven's age, and carefully built a programme of lessons to conduct after he got home from the station. Some evenings were easier than others: Eleven possessed impressive skills beyond those of the psychokinetic variety, but hadn't yet learned how to approach a problem in any way except for head-on.

Hopper tried to expand Eleven's outlook using riddles. One inclement night, he made her close her eyes as he told her a story. In this tale, Eleven and a friend (she was picturing Mike) took shelter from the rain in a cabin much like their own. The rain stopped so Eleven's friend went out to look for food. He found an arbour and, in it, an apple tree with the most delicious-looking apples he'd ever seen (Eleven didn't care much for this part, or for non-waffle food in general). The friend ate an apple from the tree and was instantly transformed into a tree himself. Shortly afterward, Eleven had to declare which tree was her friend and learned that, if she got it wrong, he would "stay as a tree... FOREVER!"

Which tree should Eleven choose?

Solution on page 177

WORD OF THE DAY
HOPPER'S CABIN

Having a "Word of the Day" thrilled Hopper when he first came up with the idea, but Eleven learned vocabulary better when he could relate it to something happening in their world. Within a couple of months, he'd run out of objects in the cabin. He couldn't even point to things outside the window because of "Don't Be Stupid" Rule number one.

Lately, Hopper had borrowed some books from former Hawkins High School classmate and current boyfriend of Joyce Byers (sigh), Bob Newby. The rebuses within the books were older than Old Man Humphrey, but Eleven's eyes lit up every time he told one. He suspected that she mostly liked the silly voices he put on.

> "WITHOUT MY FIRST, I'D HAVE YOU KNOW
> MY BEARD A FRIGHTFUL LENGTH WOULD GROW;
> DISCORDANT NOISES FROM MY NEXT
> MIGHT MAKE YOU FEEL ANNOYED AND VEXED;
> MY WHOLE'S THE BEST—YOU NEED NOT DOUBT IT,
> FOR HE'S A ROGUE WHO IS WITHOUT IT."

SOLUTION ON PAGE 177

IMMINENT DENTISTRY REQUIRED
SUBURBAN HAWKINS

Halloween was serious business in Hawkins: the one night of the year where you were allowed to accept candy from strangers – and lots of it! As the boys had decided on a group costume this year (although most people thought they'd dressed as exterminators – had they not even seen Ghostbusters?!), they agreed it was only fair if they shared their haul equally. They still felt sorry for Will, so let him keep whatever he had, but Mike gave Lucas and Dustin as many candy bars as they each already had, then Lucas gave Mike and Dustin as many as they each had, and, finally, Dustin gave Mike and Lucas as many as they each had. By the end of the candy recirculation, each boy had 24 bars.

HOW MANY CANDY BARS DID MIKE, LUCAS AND DUSTIN ORIGINALLY HAVE?

SOLUTION ON PAGE 178

TRICK OR TREAT OR TRICK
SUBURBAN HAWKINS

Mr Clarke diligently gave chocolate to all of the costumed kids who came to his door, but he had something special prepared for the Hawkins AV Club. Upon the arrival of Mike, Will, Lucas and Dustin, along with new student Maxine, he and his partner, Jen, stood side by side, holding three identical bags.

"Well, if it isn't the Ghostbusters and Michael Myers, together at last! I have a 'spook-tacular' challenge for you. One of these bags is filled to the brim with your favourite candy bars. I'm talking full-size bars here. The other two are packed with homework – algebra homework, and I'm not even your maths teacher! – that I expect on my desk by tomorrow morning. After you choose a bag, Jen will open one of the others to show you the homework within it, and then you'll have an opportunity to change your mind." After a protracted disagreement about who would get to choose, Mike was designated, partly due to his Dungeon Master skills, but also partly due to the fact that everyone except for Will voted for themselves.

Mike chose the first bag. Jen opened up the third bag to show a pile of scary-looking papers. She and Mr Clarke cackled. "If you wish to change your mind, this is the moment to do it!"

SHOULD MIKE CHANGE BAGS? AND WHY?

SOLUTION ON PAGE 178

A QUICK BITE
SUBURBAN HAWKINS

Almost as disturbing as Dustin's new pet eating his old one was the speed at which it happened – so fast, in fact, that Dustin worked out that six "catogorgons" could eat six cats in six minutes.

Now that he knew D'Artagnan wasn't alone, Dustin worried for Hawkins' feline population, which was surely doomed. If a hundred cats lived in Hawkins, he wondered, how many catogorgons would it take to eat them all in a hundred minutes at the same rate?

WHAT'S THE ANSWER TO DUSTIN'S QUESTION?

SOLUTION ON PAGE 178

The kids had abandoned the clapped-out bus only to find that the junkyard was no safer. You couldn't see the demodogs but you could hear them and, boy, were they hungry. Steve grabbed his baseball bat and strode into the mist: he may have been a terrible boyfriend but it turned out he was a pretty damn good babysitter.

Help Steve stop the onslaught while sparing his new friends. Identify the exact locations of all creatures and humans. All are positioned horizontally or vertically, and none are immediately adjacent to another one, including diagonally. The row and column numbers indicate the total segments (excluding cars) in their corresponding lines.

SOLUTION ON PAGE 179

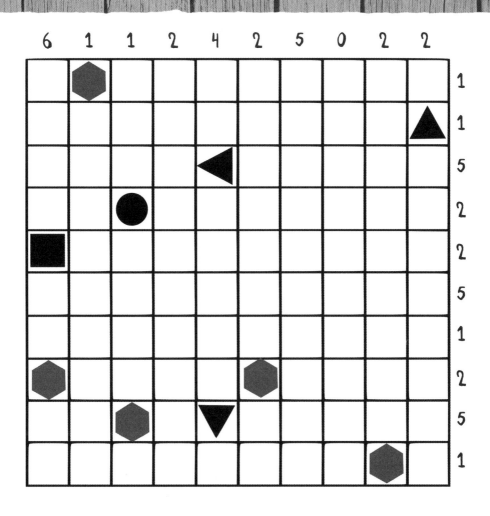

 MAX, LUCAS, DUSTIN & MIKE

 CATOGORGONS

DEMODOGS

 CARS

 DEMOGORGON

A GOOD FIRST IMPRESSION

THE BYERS' LIVING ROOM

Bob dearly wanted to connect with Jonathan and Will, and not just because of Joyce – they were good kids, and both were clearly hurting in some hidden way. Bob couldn't tell what had happened to the family. Maybe it had something to do with Joyce's freeloading ex-husband, or that week Will got lost in the woods? In any case, Bob was too timid to broach the subject. Brain teasers were his most fluent language, so that's what he tried instead. After all, what child doesn't love a diabolical puzzle?

On his first night staying over for dinner and a movie – a big occasion, with everyone on their best, most uncomfortable behaviour – Bob posed a question to each of them. To Will, he asked, "Which would you prefer: an old ten-dollar bill or a new one?" while Jonathan was struck with, "What word of five letters has only one left when two letters are removed? Hey, the answer is real heavy, man!"

Both of the boys just stared down at their TV dinners, suddenly shy. Joyce, baffled but touched, and wanting this to work, asked Bob if he had a question for her too. He did, of course – a good guest always brings something to dinner. He asked, "A farmer with a field has not enough money to buy a scarecrow, nor does he have the right equipment, yet he has no crows in his field. Why?"

WHAT WERE THE ANSWERS TO BOB'S RIDDLES?

SOLUTION ON PAGE 180

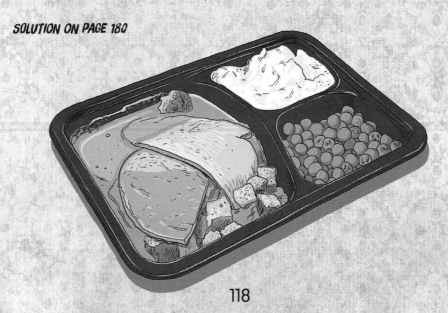

"When I was sick as a kid – and I was sick all the time as a kid – nothing made me feel better than focusing on these physical brain teasers," Bob explained to Joyce, a stack of Hi-Q boxes under his arm. Joyce had been dubious, but Will seemed to genuinely respond to the puzzles, his attention retrieved from wherever it kept going.

One day when Will was particularly impaired – shivering, his face gaunt and pale, looking at things that weren't there – Bob came around just to see him, armed with a new brainteaser that he was sure would do the trick. They didn't call him Bob the Brain for nothing.

" AT THIS MOMENT, IT IS NINE O'CLOCK AT NIGHT. CAN YOU TELL ME WHAT TIME IT WILL BE 23,999,999,992 HOURS FROM NOW?"

SOLUTION ON PAGE 180

HOW TO (DINNER) PARTY
THE BYERS' LIVING ROOM

"I wasn't always so gregarious!" Bob exclaimed as Joyce, Will and Jonathan all wondered silently whether he was gregarious at all. "I used to be very shy during my first marriage. I took pride in being able to conduct tiny dinner parties – the smallest ones possible. I remember once, I invited my father's brother-in-law, my brother's father-in-law, my father-in-law's brother and my brother-in-law's father – oh boy!"

Joyce looked up from the Ghostbusters costume she was sewing: "Bob, you were never married."

"Ssh!" he said with a grin. "Who's to say what happened in the 1970s? I was quite the rock 'n' roller, kids."

WHAT WAS THE MINIMUM POSSIBLE NUMBER OF GUESTS AT BOB'S PARTY?

SOLUTION ON PAGE 180

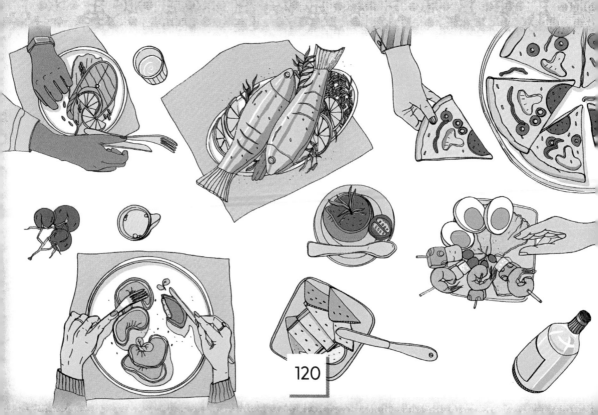

A FAINT TRACE
THE BYERS' LIVING ROOM

It wasn't until Joyce paused the video that she could see it properly. There was something there – not the image but, somehow, in the image. Even when she pressed "pause", it seemed alive, crackling with menace. She held baking paper over the television and began sketching, her son's nightmare seeping right out of the screen.

To reveal the secret image on the television, shade the grid's cells so that each column and row has continuous shaded blocks of the lengths indicated by the numbers at the start of that column or row, with at least one empty cell between each block.

SOLUTION ON PAGE 181

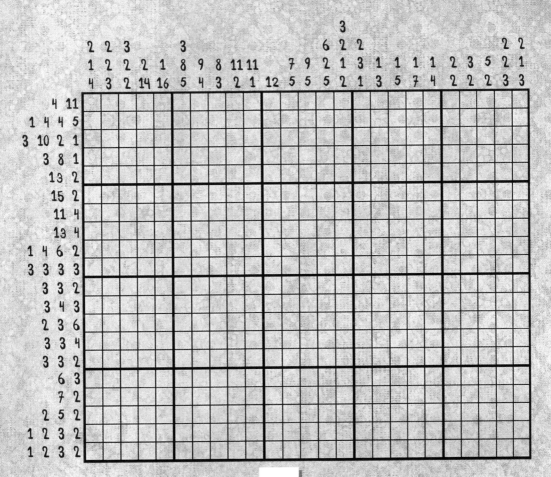

STRANGER QUIZZING
SEASON 2: EASY

1. What's the name of Dustin's ill-fated cat?

2. Who hires Murray Bauman?

3. During the second season of Stranger Things, what can be found in the Wheelers' front garden?

4. What number was given to Kali at Hawkins National Lab?

5. What's the name of Mike and Nancy's little sister?

6. What mask does Eleven wear to rob Oscar's Gas n' Go?

7. Where does Bob suggest that he, Joyce and the kids move to?

8. What role in the party does Max lobby for?

9. How does Kali respond when Axel threatens Eleven with a knife?

10. Who founded the Hawkins Middle School AV Club?

11. What's the secret of Steve hair?

SOLUTION ON PAGE 182

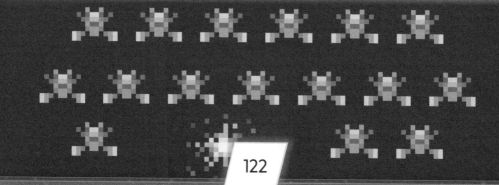

STRANGER QUIZZING
SEASON 2: HARD

1. What's the name of Dustin's replacement cat?

2. What position does Billy take from Steve at Tina's Halloween party?

3. How long does Mike try to call Eleven with his walkie-talkie for?

4. Which Ghostbuster did each of the boys dress as?

5. What did Nancy, Steve and Jonathan dress as for Halloween?

6. Who is Mr Clarke discussing when Dustin arrives late to class?

7. What book does Karen Wheeler read in the bath?

8. What's the address of Terry and Becky Ives?

9. Where did Murray Bauman previously work as an investigative journalist?

10. Who gave Bob nightmares as a child?

11. When translated from Morse code, what did Hopper's special knock for Eleven mean?

SOLUTION ON PAGE 182

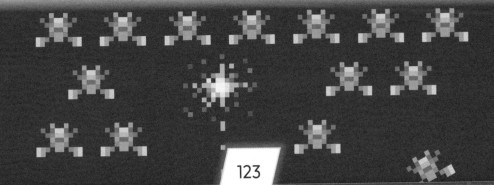

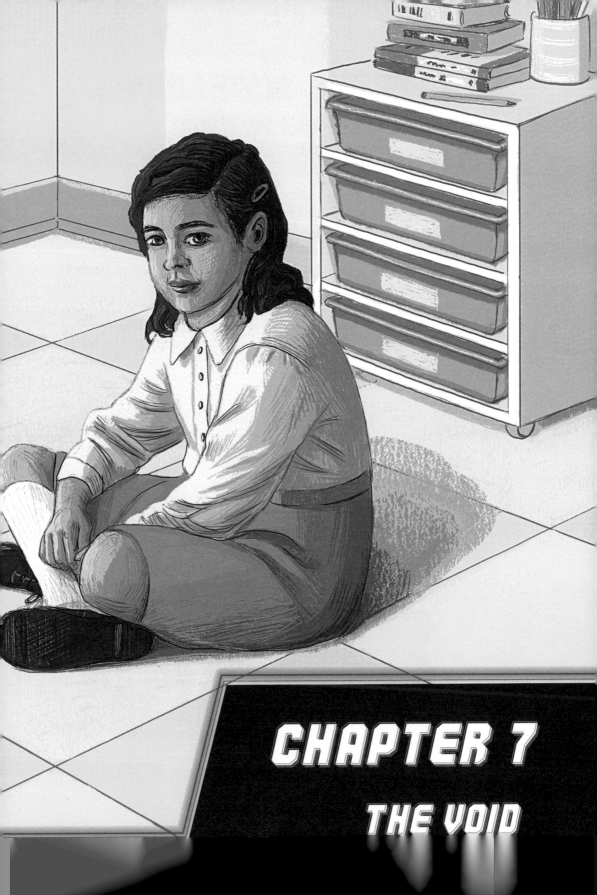

CHAPTER 7

THE VOID

BREATHE, SUNFLOWER
THE RAINBOW ROOM

When someone possesses a skill almost entirely absent from humanity, how do you teach them to use it? Dr Brenner was acutely aware that the little girl he was keeping in Hawkins National Lab had the potential to provide stronger national defence than any cruiser, tank or aircraft carrier. More effective than any military campaign, more devastating than any warhead – given half a chance, 011 might just win the Cold War by her late teens.

But it wasn't enough to merely be able to see and manipulate things from a distance; there needed to be some understanding also. Brenner would arrange particular events for 011 to spy upon, and question her on their meaning. He started slow, but the results disappointed:

"I can see two brothers. They're getting off a train, but on opposite ends. Papa, they're meeting their father. He puts his arms around them, they get into a car and go home. I don't understand."

WHO WERE THE MEN?

SOLUTION ON PAGE 183

There was something in Eleven's brain that she couldn't properly comprehend. It made her feel powerful, but she also felt like it was killing her a little each time. Whenever she approached it in her mind, something would drain out of her: the nosebleeds were only the visible signs of much larger consequences. She could feel herself restructuring.

Papa's "games" became more complicated and confusing by the day. Once, he brought her to the Rainbow Room, set up a camera, wired her to a machine, and told her a story about a comedian from Macedonia, now living with his wife in America. This man claimed that, on a recent trip to Serbia (in Yugoslavia), he'd caught rabies from a German Shepherd. He'd also met his future wife in El Salvador and won her over with her favourite non-Chinese dish. None of this made a bit of sense to Eleven but, as soon as Papa asked her a certain question, she knew the answer straight away.

WHAT WAS THE WOMAN'S FAVOURITE DISH?

SOLUTION ON PAGE 183

THREE TO THE RIGHT
THE RAINBOW ROOM

The nation's most highly advanced military structure was in place for the sole purpose of ensuring that 008 didn't escape but, on some fundamental level, Dr Brenner always understood that she would leave Hawkins National Lab as soon as she decided to. It was only a matter of will: the girl could make herself invisible to an orderly, could make a sniper believe their rifle had turned into spaghetti, could convince a sentry that she was the President and to let her out of the gate this very instant. She was the only thing stopping herself – not that she knew it yet.

Brenner's best defence against 008's inevitable departure was a heavy programme of emotional manipulation. He sought to instil a crushing guilt in her; a sense that she would harm anyone she came into contact with. One of the most effective displays of this strategy came when he brought her into the Rainbow Room and made her stand in a circle with nine others. Each person could see the entire room and everyone else. He then put a "grenade" in her hand and told her that it would go off unless she found a place to put it so that everyone except her could see it. She failed and, for months afterward, she told the on-site psychiatrist about nightmares where she was a deadly weapon about to explode, not fit to be close to anyone. It was the best possible outcome.

WHERE SHOULD KALI PLACE THE GRENADE?

SOLUTION ON PAGE 183

FOUR TO THE LEFT
THE RAINBOW ROOM

Eleven would always remember the first truly terrible thing she ever did. It happened in the Rainbow Room: Papa made her play another "game", this one requiring her to find the details of certain men. It wasn't until a few years later that Hopper off-handedly mentioned a congressman's unusual death and Eleven understood how much misery had started with her. She threw pebbles in a lake, and the ripples spoke death.

The five men all lived on Izhevsk Avenue: Jonathan, Scott, Edwin, Thomas and Charles, whose last names were Morris, Benn, Crowther, Williams and Hood. Collectively, they were graduates of Columbia, Cornell, N.Y.U., Harvard and Yale, and after college, one became a congressman, another became an engineer, one became a doctor, one became an economist, and the other became a Comptroller.

Eleven could see some facts better than others: she learned that Scott didn't go to N.Y.U. and didn't become a doctor, and neither did his friend, Mr Williams. Recently, the economist, the congressman, Jonathan, the one who attended Cornell and Edwin Crowther had lunch together. There were five men at the table. Charles was the Comptroller. Neither Thomas nor Jonathan was named Hood or Williams, and it was not one of these four who became an engineer after going to N.Y.U. Finally, the congressman and the one who went to Yale knew Thomas before he went to Harvard, and Jonathan didn't have the surname of Benn.

WHAT WAS EACH MAN'S NAME AND PROFESSION? AND WHERE DID HE GRADUATE FROM?

SOLUTION ON PAGE 183

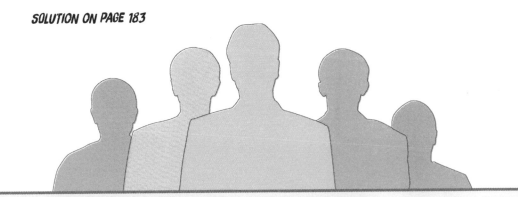

POSER ON A SCHOOL RUN
HAWKINS MIDDLE SCHOOL

Billy had few positive qualities, unless you happened to be the dissatisfied wife of Ted Wheeler, but at least he did (reluctantly) drive his sister to school every day. Confusing trite posturing for genuine rebellion, he ignored the speed limit around Hawkins Middle School, driving there at 30mph and nearly running down Max's new friends. On the way back, however, he had no-one to try to look big in front of, so made the journey at the actual speed limit of 20mph.

DISCOUNTING THE TIME HE SPENT DROPPING OFF MAX, WHAT WAS BILLY'S AVERAGE SPEED?

SOLUTION ON PAGE 183

Telling Max everything that had happened was a massive risk, but Lucas trusted her, and friends don't lie. Her response wasn't quite what he'd anticipated: she told him she liked his story but felt it was "a little derivative in parts" and "wished it had a bit more originality."

This seemed incredibly on-the-nose to Lucas, but he was more shocked by her not believing him. He asked why she'd think he could make up such a thing. "I don't know. To impress me or something? Or you're just, like, insane," she replied. "I'm sorry but it's so unlikely to have that much spooky stuff happen to one town in a week. It'd be like taking a deck of cards and drawing six reds at random, like a million to one!"

This he wouldn't stand for. "Max, that's not even remotely close to being a million to one."

WAS MAX RIGHT? WHAT'S THE PROBABILITY THAT SIX CARDS DRAWN RANDOMLY FROM A STANDARD DECK WILL ALL BE RED CARDS?

SOLUTION ON PAGE 184

A GROWING BOY
HAWKINS MIDDLE SCHOOL

"Dart's moulted again," Dustin said, his voice sheepish, excited and scared all at the same time. Mike stared at him with incredulity. "Again? It's going to be a demogorgon by recess at this rate!"

Mike wasn't far off. On the first day, Dart had increased in height by a half. That seemed understandable – it was still very young, after all – but on the second day, its height had increased by a third and, on the third day, it had increased by a quarter. What if it never ended? Would it just become a demogorgon, or keep growing forever? What was the stage after demogorgon? How big was too big for El to deal with? And how would the cats cope?

IF DART KEPT GROWING AT THE SAME RATE, HOW MANY DAYS WOULD IT TAKE TO BECOME A HUNDRED TIMES ITS ORIGINAL HEIGHT?

SOLUTION ON PAGE 184

DARTING AROUND
HAWKINS MIDDLE SCHOOL

D'Artagnan is loose!

Help the gang retrieve the budding demogorgon before it causes some real trouble.

SOLUTION ON PAGE 184

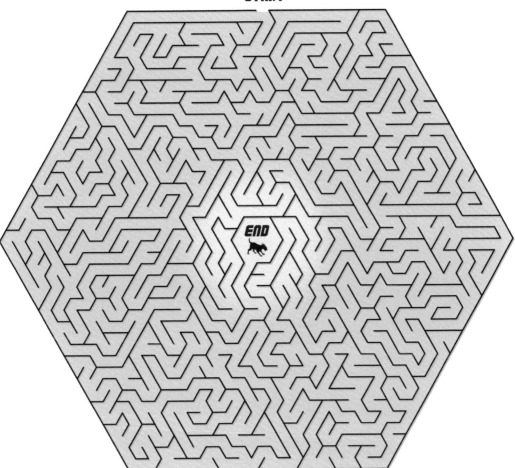

THE SPY
THE BYERS' SHED

"Will's still in there," Hopper marvelled. "He's talking to us." The boy was still possessed, but he had a tell: when presented with evidence of his most meaningful relationships, he'd involuntarily tap his thigh in Morse code. He was trying to help them, and didn't even know it. The only problem was that the messages were each, in some way, garbled, as if Will was trying to add another layer of protection to the code. This, of course, was nothing new to Joyce, who remembered her long, desperate hours in front of the alphabet wall.

A plan was swiftly formed. They'd take it in turns to remind Will how much they loved him, Dustin would decode the messages and Nancy would write them down. It was their final hope. If anyone knew how to destroy the Mind Flayer, it'd be Will.

DECIPHER WILL'S MESSAGE.

SOLUTION ON PAGE 185

"Do you remember the day Dad left? We stayed up all night building Castle Byers, just the way you drew it. And it took so long because you were so bad at hammering. You'd miss the nail every time. It started raining but we stayed out there anyway. We were both sick for a week after that, but we just had to finish it, didn't we? We just had to."

DECIPHER WILL'S MESSAGE.

SOLUTION ON PAGE 185

THE BEST FRIEND
THE BYERS' SHED

"Do you remember the day we met? It was the first day of kindergarten. I knew nobody. I had no friends and I felt so alone and so scared, but I saw you on the swings and you were alone too. You were just swinging by yourself. I walked up to you and asked if you wanted to be my friend, and you said yes. You said yes. It was the best thing I've ever done."

DECIPHER WILL'S MESSAGE.

SOLUTION ON PAGE 185

"When you turned eight, I gave you that huge box of crayons. Do you remember that? It was one hundred and twenty colours. All your friends, they got you Star Wars toys, but all you wanted to do was draw with your new colours. You drew this big spaceship, but it wasn't from a movie. It was your spaceship. A "rainbow ship" is what you called it. You must have used every colour in the box. I took that with me to Melvald's and I put it up and I told everyone who came in, 'My son drew this.' You were so embarrassed, but I was so proud. I was so, so proud."

DECIPHER WILL'S MESSAGE.

SOLUTION ON PAGE 185

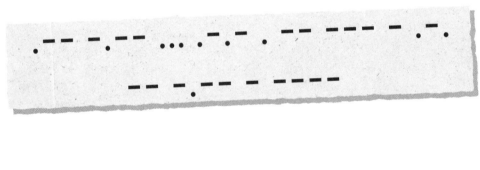

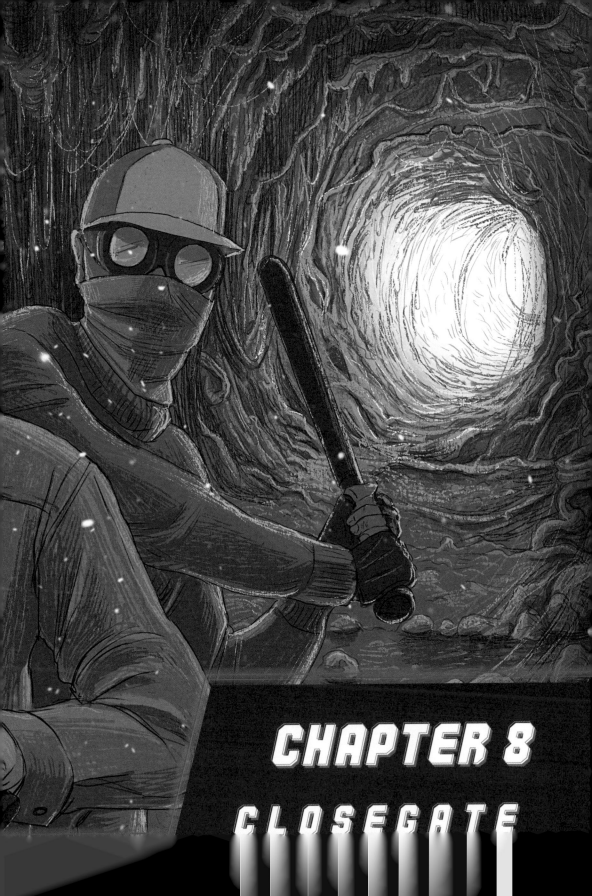

CHAPTER 8

CLOSEGATE

SELF-DESTRUCTIVE BEHAVIOUR
HNL UNDERGROUND COMPLEX

From the control booth, Dr Owens could see two things: every room in the lab complex, and that the chances of Joyce, Bob and Hopper surviving were slim-to-none. Aside from the entrance in the north-west corner – the only safe space – every lab in the complex contained a demodog.

Their sole defence was the safety feature installed shortly after the incident last November: each room was connected to its adjacent rooms by an airlock and, as Joyce, Bob and Hopper exited a demodog-contaminated room, they had to (quickly) pull a self-destruct switch, destroying the room entirely. The downside was that they couldn't re-enter a room after they'd done this. Owens needed to direct the group to the exit at the south-east corner, which was the only other room connected to the outside.

HOW CAN JOYCE, BOB AND HOPPER TRAVEL FROM THE ENTRANCE OF THE LAB COMPLEX TO THE EXIT WHILE ALSO ELIMINATING EVERY DEMODOG?

SOLUTION ON PAGE 186

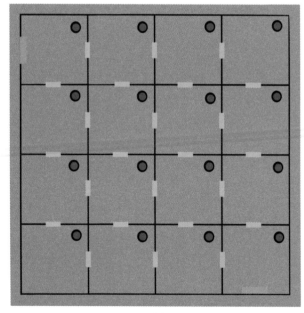

140

EASY PEASY
HNL UNDERGROUND COMPLEX

"How many are coming, Doc?" There was a pause on the line.

"All of them."

Joyce's ability to unlock the door was inhibited by the slight obstacle that every person who knew its four-digit code was in the advanced stages of being eaten alive. Bob took one look at the door's security system and told her that he could only crack it if the code began with 0, 5 or 7.

WHAT'S THE GREATEST NUMBER OF POSSIBLE FOUR-DIGIT CODES THAT BOB CAN'T CRACK?

SOLUTION ON PAGE 188

BREAKER BREAKING
HNL UNDERGROUND COMPLEX

There was, Bob had to admit, an elegant simplicity to the circumstances: he had to reset the breakers or everyone would die. His actions had never been as straightforward or important before. Do the thing, or else.

Bob passed body after body on the way to the basement. He tried not to look at them, and failed. He'd never been so afraid of anything in his life, had never even contemplated that it would be possible for him to be in a situation so terrifying, and yet he also knew he wouldn't change a moment of it. Joyce was everything to him. He reached the breaker system and understood that a whole lifetime of electronic obsession had been leading to this exact moment. He'd been teaching himself to do something incredible and hadn't realized. There was, he again had to admit, an elegant simplicity to it.

To reset the breakers, move from top left to bottom right, stopping on each square exactly once. The arrows in each square show which direction you must move in.

SOLUTION ON PAGE 188

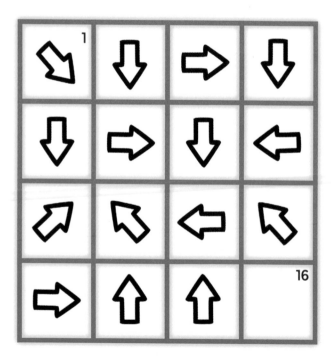

BOB NEWBY, SUPERHERO
HNL UNDERGROUND COMPLEX

He was dying, and soon. It was only a matter of seconds now until the locomotive approached. How strange to finally know that plain, mysterious fact.

Somewhere on the furthest reaches of his life, Bob's panic and fear gave way to something resembling peace. It hadn't lasted as long as he had wanted it to last and hadn't ended how he wanted it to end, but now, in his eventide, he found that he didn't mind all that much. Death is the price of admission, that's all. He thought of one last riddle, he thought of Joyce Byers, and then he left.

"If you a journey ever take,
No matter when or where.
My first would surely have to pay
Before you can get there.
My second you would scarcely see
If city through you go;
But still 'tis what I hope you are:
Few better things I know.
I say my whole with secret pain.
Though hoping soon to meet again."

SOLUTION ON PAGE 189

"SHIRLEY"
CHICAGO

"Nobody wants us around," Kali said accurately. "I know we seem a group of poorly conceived caricatures almost wholly lacking in warmth but, if you just get to know us, you'll find that we're..."

"We're exactly that!" Axel laughed, his mohawk shaking. "We're just as bad as people say we are, all right! Don't you wish you were somewhere else right now?"

Eleven found the punks alarming, with good reason – it only took them minutes to pull a switchblade on her, an actual child looking for her sister. Kali wanted Eleven to feel comfortable around her gang, but their elastic relationship to the truth wasn't making things any easier. She explained that Axel always lies on Mondays, Tuesdays and Wednesdays, and tells the truth on the other days of the week. Mick, on the other hand, lies on Thursdays, Fridays and Saturdays, but tells the truth for the rest of the week. As soon as she'd said this, Axel and Mick both stated that yesterday was one of their lying days, before crowing mean-spiritedly.

Eleven wore her familiar look of blankness until she remembered the lessons with Hopper back at the cabin: she realized that, from their two statements, she could work out the truth.

WHAT DAY WAS IT?

SOLUTION ON PAGE 189

DIVIDING THE SPOILS, SPOILING THE DIVIDE

THE BYERS' SHED

Kali told Eleven that the punks were much worse before she joined them, which, for some reason, was meant to be consoling. Back then, it was just Mick, Axel and Funshine, and they couldn't trust each other or even steal well. Their biggest ever score was a pile of Twinkies from a gas station. They didn't bother to count their loot, but saw that it was between 50 and 100 cakes.

The three punks agreed that, the next morning, they would divide the Twinkies between them, which would have been fine except that, during the night, Axel took his one-third share of the pile and hid it, afraid that his friends would cheat him. As there was a Twinkie more than the quantity that could be equally split into thirds, he tossed one out of the window and went to sleep. Later, a similarly paranoid Funshine did exactly the same thing. He took a third of the Twinkies in the pile and, after also finding that there was one too many cakes to be equally divided into thirds, launched the extra Twinkie at a hapless pigeon. Finally, Mick awoke and took the same action as her ostensible partners, hiding a third of the remaining Twinkie pile and feeding the extra Twinkie to that same pigeon.

Once the morning finally arrived, the punks saw that the pile had shrunk dramatically, but nobody said anything as they all afraid of what would happen if they owned up. They divided the pile in three and ditched the extra Twinkie. None of them ever knew the extent of their mutual duplicity until Kali made them confess later, threatening them with flaming spiders if they didn't.

HOW MANY TWINKIES WERE IN THE ORIGINAL PILE?

SOLUTION ON PAGE 189

AN ELEVEN AND AN EIGHT
CHICAGO

When they weren't plundering their way across the greater Chicago area, the punks spent most of their time playing cards, or trying to avoid playing cards; as Mick put it, one hand leads to two hands, two hands lead to three and, before you know it, you're as broke as Axel.

Eleven couldn't fathom the game that Axel, Mick, Dottie and Funshine were playing, but it involved each person playing with a two-card hand. In the latest round, each person held two cards in the same suit, and no player received cards in the same suit as any other player. The first cards were an Ace, a King, a Queen and a Jack, while the second cards were a Ten, a Nine, an Eight and a Seven.

Curious about Eleven's powers – specifically, how far they might be pushed for their benefit – Kali asked Eleven to tell her which cards each player received. Eleven cleared her mind and, immediately, some information came to her. Dottie and Funshine each had a picture card: one of them had Spades and the other had a Nine. The player with the King didn't have Hearts or the Seven, and neither did Axel, while Mick didn't have the Jack or the Eight. Dottie sat to the right of Mick, who sat to the right of the player with Diamonds, who sat to the right of the player with the Queen of Clubs. Finally, the Jack, the Ten, the Eight and the Diamonds were in four different hands.

WHAT CARDS DID EACH PLAYER HOLD?

SOLUTION ON PAGE 189

CRIME DOES PAY, VERY SLIGHTLY
CHICAGO

"We're only stealing from the war-criminal billionaires who own this place," Kali reassured Eleven, which she could believe so long as she didn't spend too long looking at the hand-painted sign that read "OSCAR'S GAS N' GO". The robbery itself went relatively well – a new pair of sunglasses, some beer, waffles – until the attendant, Darrel, pulled a gun on them, although he arguably seemed more scared than they were. Later, in the van, Axel mentioned that he'd read in a free magazine from the airport that 78 per cent of all gas-station owners are armed, and 35 per cent of all gas-station owners have children. He was clearly just trying to rile the others, but it worked, for a little while, at least.

AT THE GANG'S NEXT GAS-STATION ROBBERY, WHAT'S THE PROBABILITY THAT THE OWNER WILL BE UNARMED AND HAVE NO CHILDREN?

SOLUTION ON PAGE 189

Way to Go
The Tunnels

No matter what dumb sports metaphor Steve was using to try to dissuade them, Max, Lucas, Dustin and Mike weren't going to just stand around while Eleven was in danger: a party member required assistance, and it was their duty to provide that assistance.

Using Will's sketches of the vines, help the group plot a journey from the tunnel entrance (marked on the grid by a blue square) to the hub (marked with a red square).

To reveal the tunnels, shade the grid's cells so that each column and row has continuous shaded blocks (including the coloured squares) of the lengths indicated by the numbers at the start of that column or row, with at least one empty cell between each block.

SOLUTION ON PAGE 190

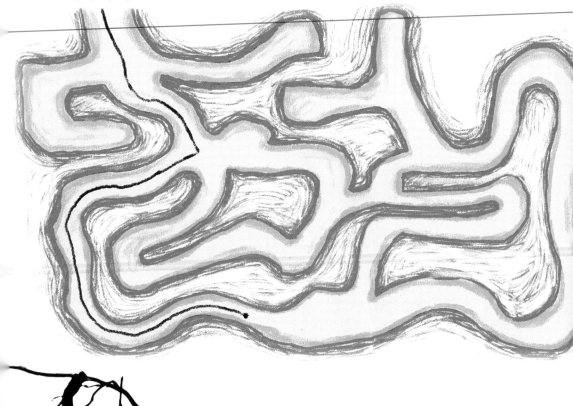

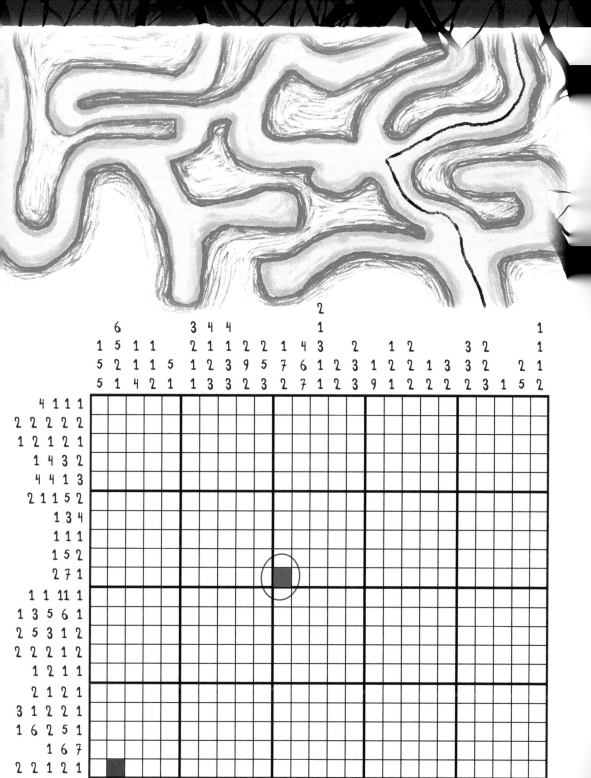

"DRENCH IT"
THE TUNNELS

Will's sketches hadn't done justice to quite how horribly alive the tunnels felt. They groaned, they pulsated, they oozed disgusting spores that would get right in your mouth if you weren't careful (or if you were Dustin). Even if the party weren't being hunted down by demodogs, lingering wasn't advisable unless you were hoping to become a permanent resident or a pile of black sludge.

Help Steve, Max, Lucas, Dustin and Mike find the hub and burn it down.

SOLUTION ON PAGE 191

START

END

HEALING A RIFT
THE TUNNELS

Eleven floated in the air and every light in Hawkins shone with her. She threw her arms toward the Gate, thinking of the people in her life. Hopper. Mama. Kali. Lucas. Dustin. Aunt Becky. Joyce. Nancy. Jonathan. Mike.

All Hopper could do was try to help, which meant holding the demodogs off for as long as possible. The chief had great aim but the monsters came from every angle, providing him an equal chance of hitting or missing them. Hopper would give his life for that girl if he had to, but not here and not today – he'd make sure of it.

IF HOPPER SHOOTS AT SIX DEMODOGS, WHAT'S THE PROBABILITY OF HIM HITTING AT LEAST ONE?

SOLUTION ON PAGE 191

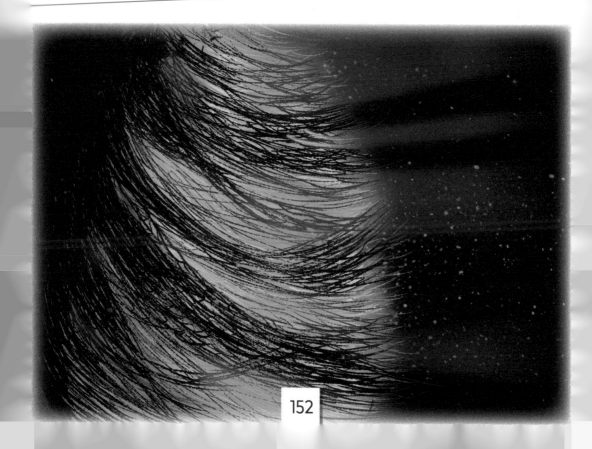

THE TUNNELS

"You did good, kid. You did so good."

The lift carried them slowly up to Hawkins. Maybe everything really was going to be OK. Who knew? The Gate was closed – that was something. Hopper looked down at Eleven, slumped against his shins. The last time she'd defeated unspeakable evil, the effort caused her to disassemble and reappear in an entirely different place, so he couldn't imagine the strength it had taken to stay here with him. He poked the top of her head.

"Hey, kiddo, I never told you today's word of the day."
"Oh?"
He'd memorized an actual poem for this very event. Hopper was changing – or changing back – into the sort of man who'd learn a poem just to make his daughter smile.
His daughter, yes.

"Deceitful, godless, prone to deeds accursed,
Must be the man whose ways are not my first.
When sterile winter holds its chilly reign,
My second may be seen on yonder plain.
Those who the path of honesty forsake,
My whole at last will surely overtake."

WHAT WAS THE WORD OF THE DAY?

SOLUTION ON PAGE 191

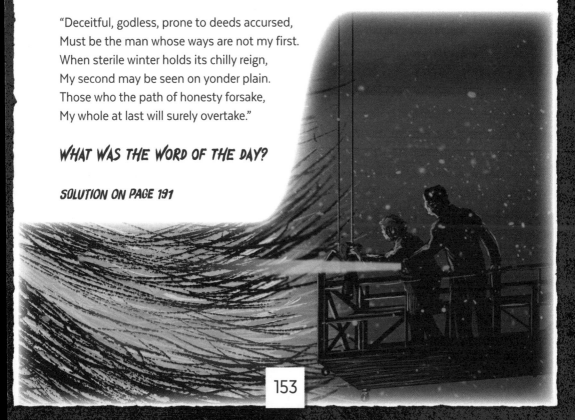

ANSWERS

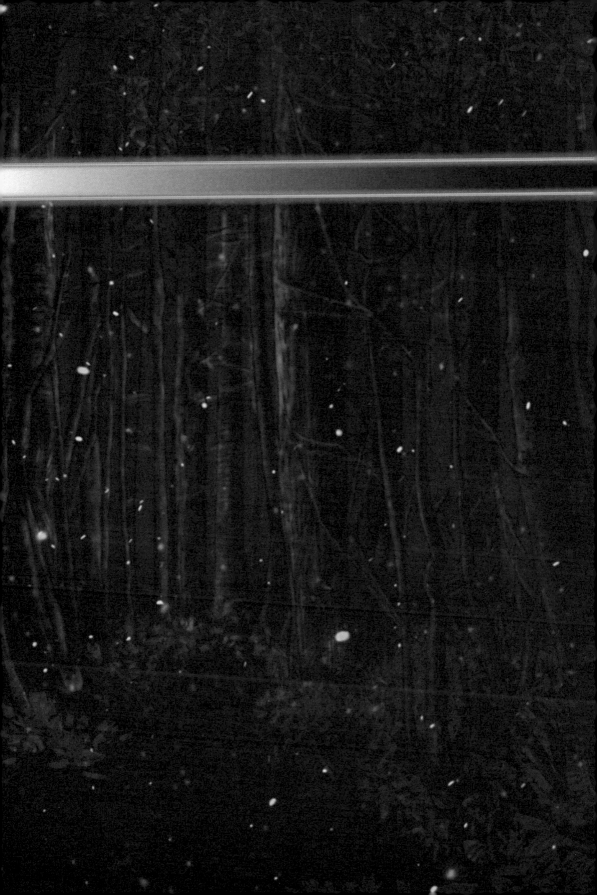

ANSWERS

SEASON 1
CHAPTER ONE: THE VANISHING OF WILL BYERS

1 – Will Beats the Demogorgon (I)
The probability that Will's number is higher is 19 out of 40. The chances that both numbers are the same is 1 out of 20, which means the probability that they're different is 19 out of 20. If they're different, the chances are even that Will's roll is greater, so the total probability is one half of 19 out of 20, which is also 19 out of 40.

2 – The Bloodstone Pass
"Holes."

3 – All the Range on Maple Street
There are 12 houses on Maple Street, including Mike's, so he could theoretically reach 10 of them (not including his own) with his Supercom. However, the Wheelers also have a telephone, so he could possibly contact all 11 of them if they also had phones.

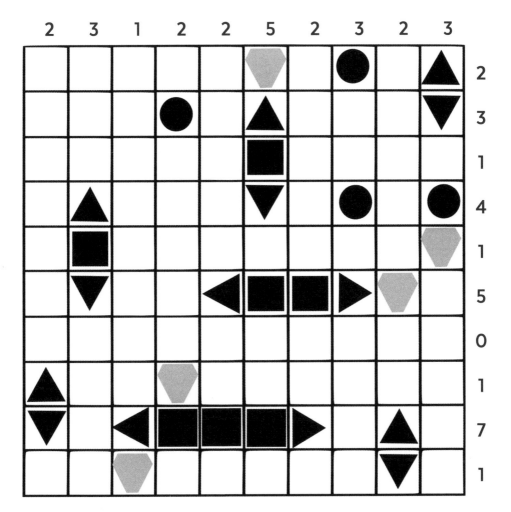

START

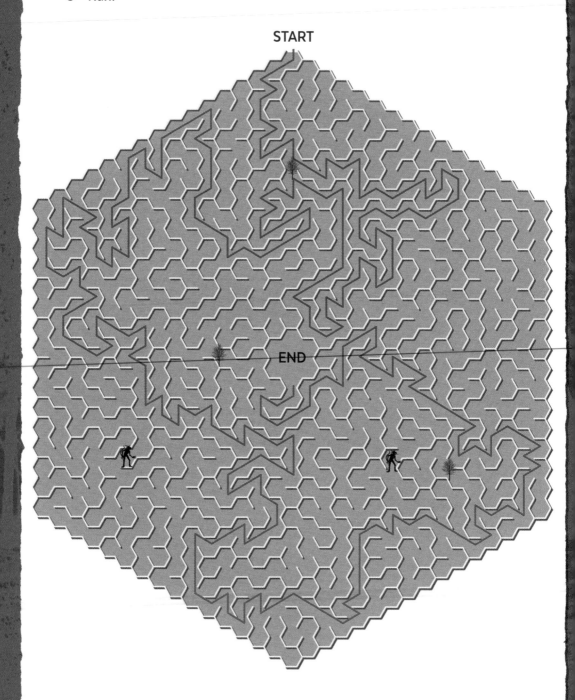

END

6 - The Vanishing
It was a snowball and, therefore, both it and the incriminating wet patch were gone by the time her parents got home.

7 - Operation Mirkwood
62 and a half wafers.

8 - Trouble Down the Line
Whichever train is travelling against the spin of the earth will wear its wheels out first, as it has less centrifugal forces working on it.

9 - Long Hours at Hawkins Public Library
The answer to the first question was once, because, the next time, you'd be taking 5 from 20.

The answer to the second question is that one of the books has zero words and is about nothing. As the number of books is greater than the number of words in the largest book (with no two books having the same number of words), the number of books will always be one more than the number of words in the largest book. No matter how many books are in the library, there will always be books with each possible number of words less than the largest book, and there will always be a book that had no words (to increase the total number).

10 - Across the Counter of Melvald's
Donald gave Joyce a $96 advance.

11 - Hunting Season
The three fractions were 40/60 for torches, 45/60 for gasoline and 48/60 for bear traps. Add together 40, 45 and 48 and deduct twice 60 and the result is 13, the minimum number for every 60 customers. As the minimum of customers who bought all 3 items was 26, the total number of customers that week must have been 120.

12 - The Body
Joyce should ask the second coroner. The first man would give the answer yes whether he was telling the truth or not. The second man, therefore, said that the first man would say yes, meaning he's telling the truth and the first man is a liar.

ROANE COUNTY
CORONER

13 – Under the Skin
The man should drink from the Frigid, Evolve or Airplane bottles to be poisoned.

14 – Grim Argot
"Har" is the only common code word in the first two phrases, while "good" is the only common one in its English form, so "har" means "good". In the following two phrases, "dret" is used and its English translations share "friends", so "dret" means "friends". The first and third phrases both share "yul" so it must mean "admire", leaving "illik" to mean "perimeters". "Camb" must, therefore, mean "disarm" in the second phrase, and "loppe" means "quietly". For Eleven to say, "Disarm perimeters quietly," then – assuming the syntax follows English – she should say, "Camb illik loppe."

15 – Tatishchevo

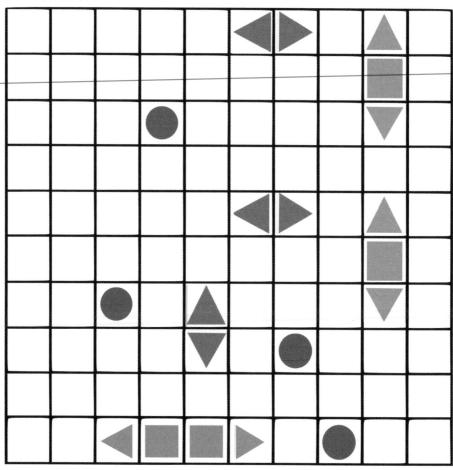

16 – Another Time Another Place

Dr Brenner can find the bearded man at Camp Hero at 20:15 on 6 November 1983.

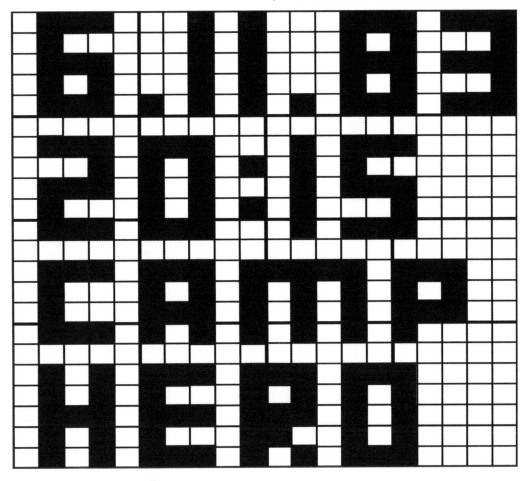

17 – Upside Down Password

1961.

18 – The Rule of Law

There were no handshakes as one of the two
people would always be taller than the other.

19 – Losing Time

After showing the correct time at the start of the trip, Mike's watch won't appear to be accurate again for 720 days (60 minutes per hour x 12 hours), at which point it will be exactly 12 hours behind but will still display the correct time. Lucas's watch will suffer the same fate in the other direction, being wrong for 720 days until it is momentarily accurate again. Both watches are equally likely to be incorrect, meaning that Dustin's broken one – which is right twice a day, every 12 hours – is the most likely to be accurate.

20 – Unconventional Gifts

"Eleven has 18." Each letter in the person's name is equal to three of "them", therefore, Eleven, with just 6 letters in her name, has 18 of "them".

21 – A Small Crime Wave

Noah and Arthur stole Phil Larson's gnomes. Hopper told all three that they were idiots and sent them on their way.

22 – Eleanor Gillespie's Head

Hopper could find Eleanor at the Hawk Theatre, although her experience may have put her off venues named after medium-sized birds of prey. Bev and Doris worked for Hawkins Water & Sewer Authority.

23 – Slow Century

Hopper. Powell arrested more people than Callahan and Hopper arrested more people than Powell, therefore, he caught more than either of them and, as Callahan had arrested more people than Simmons, Hopper had beaten him too.

24 – Heavy Weather

The odd weather had been going on for 18 days. There are 23 fine half-days and 13 rainy half-days, giving 18 days in total.

25 – Stranger Quizzing, Season 1: Easy

1. Matt and Ross Duffer.
2. Because she cuts her hand while trying to open a beer can with a knife.
3. The Millennium Falcon.
4. Chocolate pudding.
5. "Should I Stay or Should I Go" by the Clash.
6. The U.S. Department of Energy.
7. She's had another child.
8. A new camera.
9. His father Lonny made him shoot a rabbit.
10. R I G H T H E R E
11. "Mouth breather."

26 – Stranger Quizzing, Season 1: Hard

1. 6 November 1983
2. Will has a *Jaws* poster, Jonathan has a poster for *The Evil Dead,* and Mike has a poster for *The Dark Crystal* (the poster for *The Thing* is in Mike's basement, not his bedroom).
3. 22 inches and 10 times bigger, which seems unlikely.
4. Roane County, Indiana.
5. Cleidocranial dysplasia.
6. Going to the cinema to watch *All The Right Moves.*
7. Jennifer Hayes.
8. *Anne of Green Gables.*
9. X-Men #134.
10. Project MKUltra.
11. $22.56

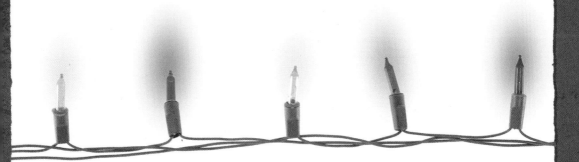

27 - A Couple of Tall Boys

Only one statement is true so, if Steve is right that he's had a hundred beers since the summer, Tommy's statement that he's had fewer would be false, but Nancy's statement that he's had at least one would be true, and this isn't possible. If Nancy's statement is true, Steve and Tommy's statements couldn't both be false as they contradict each other – Steve couldn't have had both more and fewer than one hundred beers. Therefore, Tommy must be telling the truth that Steve has had fewer than a hundred beers but, as Nancy must also be wrong, Steve hasn't had at least one beer: he's had none.

28 - In the Drink

Steve's aim is, ultimately, to leave Tommy with five cans so that, no matter how many beers he drinks at that point, Steve will be able to leave him with a single can. To get to that stage, Steve can start the contest by drinking two beers, leaving Tommy with nine cans. This will mean that regardless of whether Tommy then drinks one, two or three beers (leaving eight, seven or six cans), Steve will be able to drink enough to leave five beers remaining.

29 - Low-light

While the question seems to give insufficient information, Nancy's mood isn't pertinent to the answer: if she is glum, a glum person is looking at a non-glum person (Nancy looking at Steve) and, if she isn't, a glum person is still looking at a non-glum person (Jonathan looking at Nancy).

START

END

31 – The Rainbow Speaks

Will's message is, as stated, in Latin. The lit-up letters are ACMRSTU, clearly an anagram. Their order is determined by the hint in the title: the order of a rainbow (Red, Orange, Yellow, Green, Blue, Indigo, Violet). Once the letters are in order, the lights read: CASTRUM. This translates into English as "castle"; Will is talking of Castle Byers.

32 – Mixed Results

The lit-up letters are now AILMUX. However, red appears twice, and orange, green, indigo and violet not at all. Instead there is a brown and blue-green – the colours you obtain upon mixing orange and violet, and green and indigo. This indicates A and M are the first and last letters, while U and I appear twice, in their respective positions. Following this logic, AUXILIUM can be obtained, which translates to "help" in English.

33 – A Stern Message

The lit-up letters are now CEILMPRU. Following the same logic as before, U appears twice as a mixture of orange and green, while red appears twice, as does orange (albeit once in the mixture). Placing the letters reveals MULUCIREP. When reversed (or read "astern") the Latin reads PERICULUM, which translates into "danger".

34 – Mounting Disarray

This final message is in disarray; it is an anagram. The different colours indicate the number of times a letter appears: red = 1, orange = 2. The letters are therefore EEIIMNSV. This can be rearranged into INVENIS ME which translates as "find me".

35 – A Shortfall on the Register

There are 720 different permutations: the result of 6 x 5 x 4 x 3 x 2 x 1. The first person on the row can be any of the 6 students, giving 6 options, while the next is chosen from 5 options and the next from 4 options and so on. This is called factorial 6, also printed as 6!. It's a good thing the class size was small: if there were 10 students in the row, there would be more than 3,628,800 ways of arranging them.

37 – Piecing It All Together – Two possible answers.

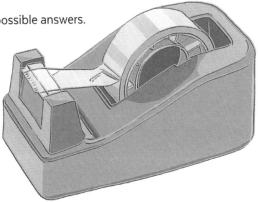

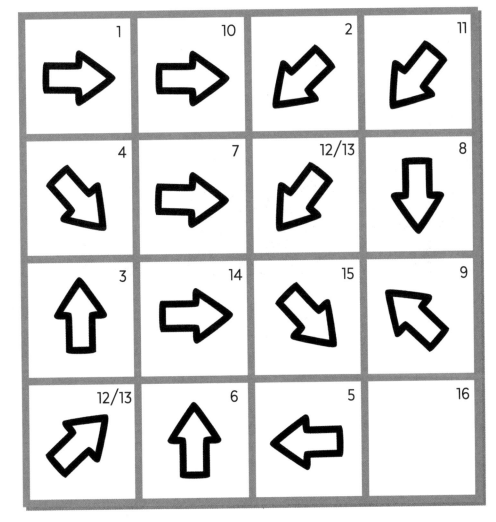

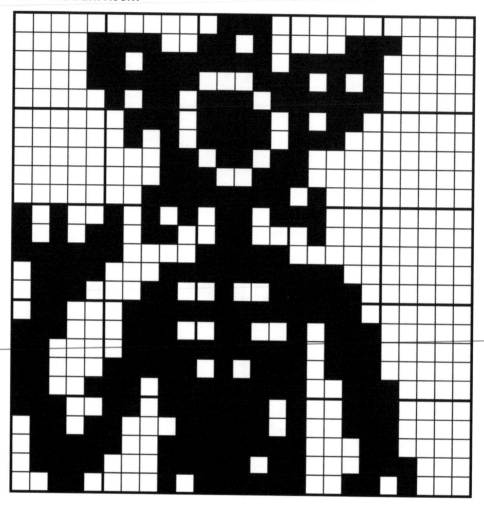

CHAPTER FOUR: LIFE UPSIDE DOWN

39 – Waffling On
The woman entered the supermarket with $99.98 (and left with $49.99).

40 – The Incapacitating Agent
If you read the note backward and ignore the spaces and punctuation, it says: LOOK UP ITS IN THE CEILING LIGHT OF THE TRAILER.

41 – A Bit of a Leap
Jump from the bottom rung.

42 – Flipping Angry

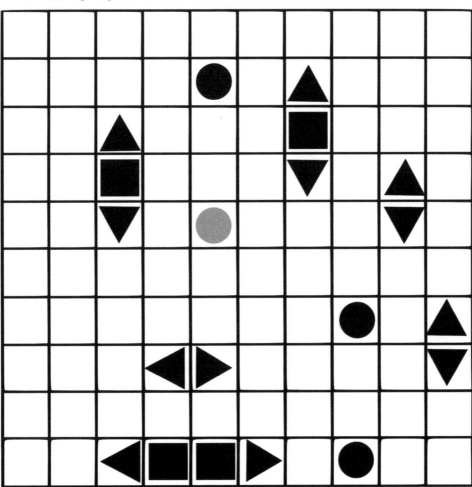

43 – Justice for Barb

The time, correct to the nearest second, was 27 minutes and 42 seconds after 6 o'clock.

44 – Going South

Shepard had travelled 18 miles from the gate. If x is the distance between the two places, then Shepard walked for $x/3$ hours and his body was pulled for $x/9$ hours, which means $x/3 + x/9 = 8$. Therefore $x = 18$.

45 – Will Beats the Demogorgon (II)

There are only three possible outcomes: Will hits the Demogorgon with his first shot and misses with his second, Will misses with his first shot and hits with his second, or Will makes both shots. Therefore, the probability of him striking the Demogorgon both times is 1/3.

46 – Visiting the Library

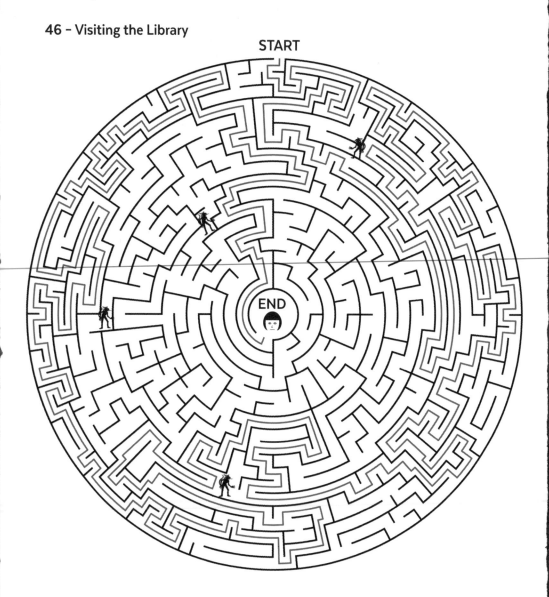

47 - A New Order

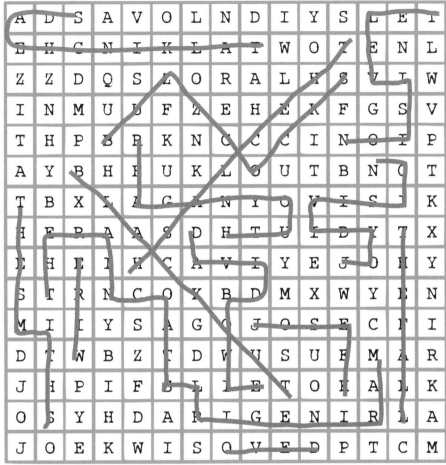

48 – Mr Clarke on Tour

Lucas, Mike and Dustin would hear the music first – radio waves travel at the speed of light, so they would reach the ham shack before the sound travels to Mr Clarke in the stalls.

49 – Paper Plates and String

It seems counter-intuitive, but the bicycle would move backward (and the pedal would move anti-clockwise). While the pedal travels backward relative to the bike during normal use, relative to the ground, it is moving forward. The pedal and the bike always move together so, if the pedal is pulled backward, the bike moves backward too.

50 – No More

A nest.

51 - Things Growing in Hawkins

The infection won't reach all of the pumpkins. In order to do so, the length of its final boundary would need to be 40, as an infected 10 x 10 field's perimeter is 10 + 10 + 10 + 10 = 40. A single infected pumpkin has a perimeter of 4, which means the perimeter of 9 rotten pumpkins would be 36 at most (4 x 9). The perimeter doesn't increase as the infection grows: if an uninfected pumpkin is infected by two pumpkins, say, two of its sides are absorbed into the infected area, and the other two become part of the perimeter of the infected area – the perimeter loses two and gains two, resulting in a net change of zero. This means that a perimeter of 9 infected pumpkins will always be 36 at most. It can't reach 40 as it cannot increase and, therefore, can't spread to every pumpkin in the field.

52 - Squash Crime

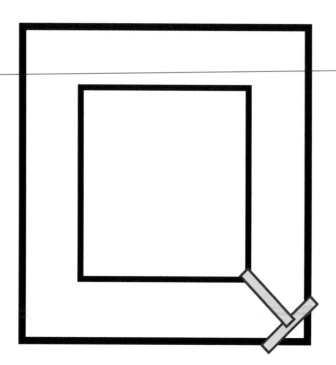

53 – A Short-lived Heirloom
First place: Eugene McCorkle – Rouge Vif D'Etampes
Second place: Merrill – Blue Lakota
Third place: Pete Freeling – Jarrahdale
Fourth place: Merrill – Connecticut Field Pumpkin
Fifth place: Jack O'Dell – Speckled Hound
Sixth place: Rick Neary – Queensland Blue

54 – Out Standing in his Field
The pumpkin weighed 30 pounds. The weight (W) equals $10 + \frac{1}{2}(10) + \frac{1}{2}W$, therefore $15 = \frac{1}{2}W$ and W = 30 pounds.

55 – Pulling Weeds
The actual numbers can vary but the key is to put cages inside of cages: for example, Teddy could put nine tendrils each in three cages, and then put those three inside a fourth, larger cage.

56 – Long Night
As the tendrils double in quantity each minute, the container was half full at 22:59.

57 – Breeding Frenzy
By the end of seven generations, 335,923,200,000,000 spores would have been produced.

1 April: A female spore produces 120 eggs. Mid-April, 120 spores will hatch. Female spores: 60

20 April: 60 female spores produce 120 eggs each. Beginning of May, 60 x 120 = 7,200 spores will hatch. Female spores: 3,600

10 May: 3,600 female spores produce 120 eggs each. Mid-May, 3,600 x 120 = 432,000 spores will hatch. Female spores: 216,000

30 May: 216,000 females spores produce 120 eggs each. Beginning of June, 216,000 x 120 = 25,920,000 spores will hatch. Female spores: 12,960,000

19 June: 12,960,000 female spores produce 120 eggs each. End of June, 12,960,000 x 120 = 1,555,200,000 spores will hatch. Female spores: 777,600,000

9 July: 777600000 female spores produce 120 eggs each. Mid-July, 777,600,000 x 120 = 93,312,000,000 spores will hatch. Female spores: 46,656,000,000

29 July: 46,656,000,000 female spores produce 120 eggs each. Beginning of August, 46,656,000,000 x 120 = 5,598,720,000,000 spores will hatch. Female spores: 2,799,360,000,000

18 August: 2,799,360,000,000 female spores produce 120 eggs each. Last week of August, 2,799,360,000,000 x 120 = 335,923,200,000,000 spores will hatch.

58 – A Life or Death Situation
The question presents two options.
The first option shows that it's possible for a kid to be a Reese's Pieces fan but, in the second option, we see that this is not definite. Therefore, the conclusion is false.

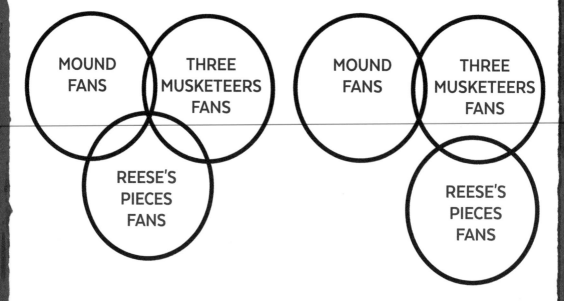

59 – Old Man Humphrey
Lucas worked for 16 minutes and 40 seconds, and idled for 13 minutes and 20 seconds.

60 – Mr Target!
To beat the game would cost Will six quarters: he must hit 17 four times and 16 twice.

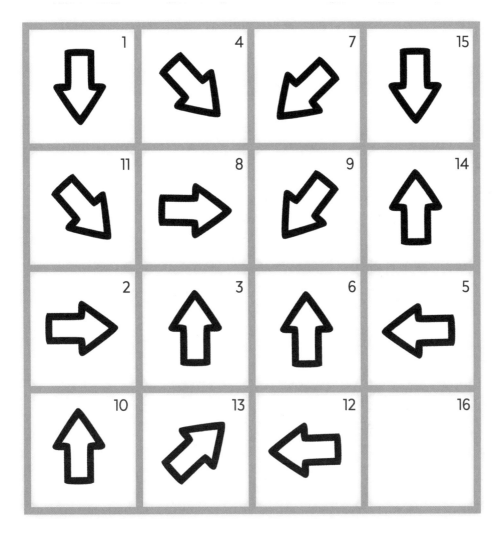

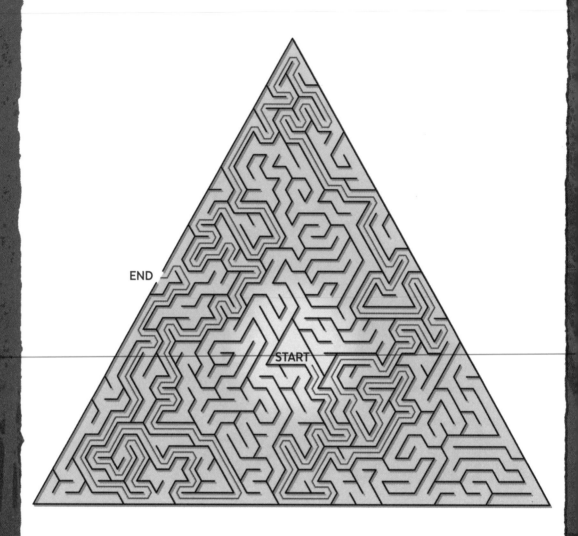

63 – The "Don't Be Stupid" Rules

The problem gives two equations, which can be merged together to solve the problem. Let "t" be the number of tripwires and "d" be the number of doors:

$t = d + 1$

$d = t/2 + 1$

$d - 1 = t/2$

$2d - 2 = t$

$2d - 2 = d + 1$

$2d - d = 1 + 2$

$d = 3$

If we substitute 3 for "d" in the original equation, it shows that "t" equals 4, meaning that there are three doors and four tripwires.

64 – Bored Games

Eleven must win 90 per cent of the remaining games. If Eleven wins 60 per cent of one-third of the games, it is the same as winning 20 per cent of all the games. Therefore:

20 per cent + 2/3x = 80 per cent

2/3x = 60 per cent

2x = 180 per cent

x = 90 per cent

65 – Night School

As the rain stopped shortly before Eleven's friend left the cabin, she should choose whichever tree isn't wet.

66 – Word of the Day

"Honesty."

67 - Imminent Dentistry Required
Mike had 39 candy bars, Lucas had 21 and Dustin had 12:

24 + 24 + 24 = 72
12 + 12 + 48 = 72
6 + 42 + 24 = 72
39 + 21 + 12 = 72

68 - Trick or Treat or Trick
Even though the result is uncertain, Mike made the more informed decision: switching his choice makes the probability of choosing the right bag as two-thirds. There are three possible configurations of candy and homework:

Bag 1: Candy; Bag 2: Homework; Bag 3: Homework
Jen opens Bag 2 or 3. If Mike switches, he loses and, if he doesn't switch, he wins.

Bag 1: Homework; Bag 2: Candy; Bag 3: Homework
Jen opens Bag 3. If Mike switches, he wins and, if he doesn't switch, he loses.

Bag 1: Homework; Bag 2: Homework; Bag 3: Candy
Jen opens Bag 2. If Mike switches, he wins and, if he doesn't switch, he loses.

By changing his selection, Will is now in the position of having two out of three chances of winning the candy and one out of three of getting the homework, while, if he doesn't switch, those odds are reversed.

69 - A Quick Bite
If six catogorgons can eat six cats in six minutes, six catogorgons can eat one cat in one minute. Therefore, six catogorgons would eat a hundred cats in a hundred minutes.

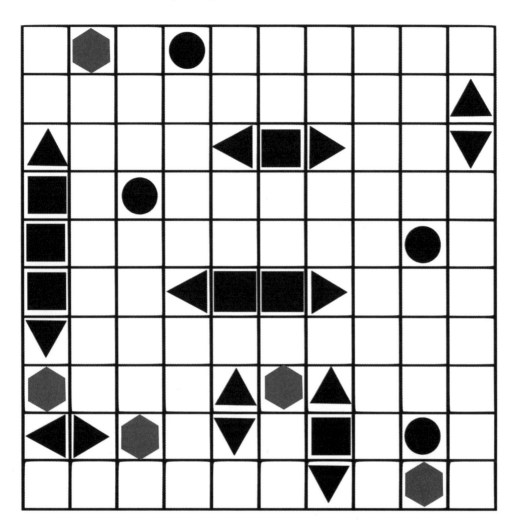

71 – A Good First Impression
1. An old $10 bill is usually preferable to a new $1 bill (a "new one").
2. "Stone."
3. The farmer has no vegetables in his field.

72 – Bob the Brain
24 billion hours later, it would be 9 p.m., so eight hours before that would be 1 p.m.

73 – How to (Dinner) Party
The minimum number is one if enough family conditions are met (and assuming that Bob lived in a state with legal cousin marriage). His mother must have two brothers (brother 1 and 2). Bob must also have a brother who married the daughter of brother 1, a cousin, and a sister who married the son of brother 1. Bob would be married to the daughter of brother 2. This means that brother 1 is Bob's father's brother-in-law, Bob's brother's father-in-law, Bob's father-in-law's brother and Bob's brother-in-law's father, and the only guest at a presumably very awkward dinner party.

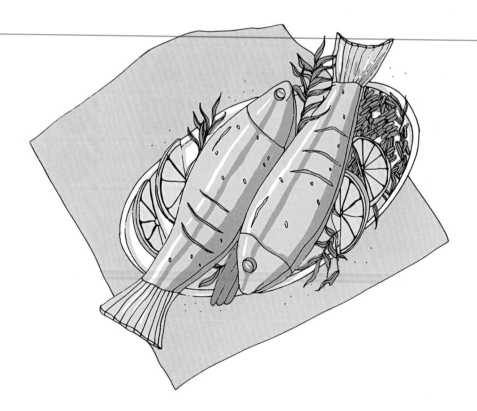

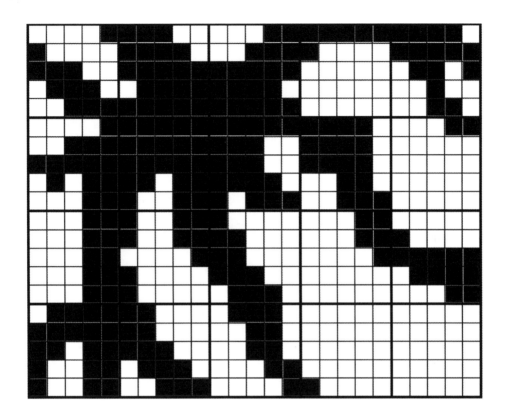

75 – Stranger Quizzing, Season 2: Easy

1. Mews and Tews.
2. Barb's parents.
3. A "Reagan/Bush '84" yard sign.
4. 008.
5. Holly Wheeler.
6. A baby face.
7. Maine.
8. A "Zoomer".
9. She gives him a hallucination of spiders running up his hand.
10. Bob Newby.
11. Four puffs of Farrah Fawcett hairspray.

76 – Stranger Quizzing, Season 2: Hard

1. Tews.
2. Keg King.
3. 352 days.
4. Will dressed as Egon Spengler, Dustin dressed as Ray Stantz, and both Mike and Lucas dressed as Peter Venkman.
5. Nancy and Steve dressed as Rebecca De Mornay and Tom Cruise in Risky Business, and Jonathan dressed as "a guy who hates parties".
6. Phineas Gage.
7. *Heart of Thunder* by Johanna Lindsey.
8. 515 Larrabee Road.
9. The *Chicago Sun-Times*.
10. Mr Baldo the clown.
11. US.

77 – Breathe, Sunflower
The men were monks, newly posted to a monastery, and their "father" was the abbot.

78 – Rainbow, 450
Each sentence refers to an anagram of the first country mentioned in that sentence, so the wife is a "salad lover", an anagram of El Salvador.

79 – Three to the Right
Kali should place the grenade on her own head.

80 – Four to the Left
Jonathan Morris, Yale, doctor.
Scott Hood, Columbia, congressman.
Edwin Crowther, NYU, engineer.
Thomas Benn, Harvard, economist.
Charles Williams, Cornell, comptroller.

81 – Poser on a School Run
The average speed is 24mph – more time is spent driving at 20mph than at 30mph.
To work this out, "d" is the distance to the school, "T" is the time it gets to get there, "t" is the time it takes to return, and "A" is the average speed. Distance equals rate x time:
d = 20T
T = d/20
d = 30t
t = d/30
As we now have expressions for "T" and "t", an equation can describe the round trip:
2d = A(T + t)
2d = A(d/20 + d/30)
2d = A(3d/60 + 2d/60)
2d = A(5d/60)
A = 120d/5d
A = 24

82 – Lucas Faces the Critics

(26/52) x (25/51) x (24/50) x (23/49) x (22/48) x (21/47) = 253/22372, which is a little better than 1 in 90.

83 – A Growing Boy

It would take Dart 198 days to grow to 100 times its original size. If, for example, it was 1 foot tall when Dustin found it, on the end of the first day, it would be 1½ feet tall. On the next day, it would gain a third of 1½ feet (½ foot), making it 2 feet tall, and on the day after that, it would gain a quarter of 2 feet (also ½ foot). This means it would gain ½ foot each day. After 198 days, it would have gained 99 feet, making it 100 times as tall as on the first day.

84 – Darting Around

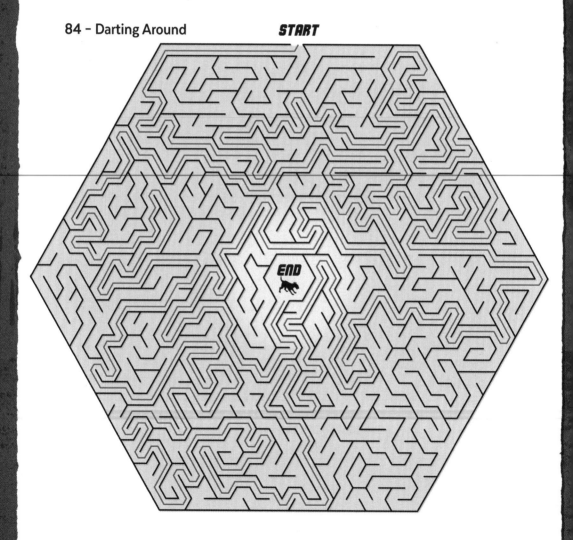

85 – The Spy

Read backwards, the Morse Code spells S T I L L H E R E.

86 – The Older Brother

Read backwards, the Morse Code spells L O V E Y O U M O M A N D J O N A T H A N.

87 – The Best Friend

The Morse Code here is in the correct order, but the dots represent dashes and the dashes represent dots. The message reads D O N T L E T M E K N O W W H E R E I A M.

88 – Mom

The dots and dashes are reversed, but here, the message is also spelled backwards. It reads: H E L I K E S I T C O L D.

89 - Self-destructive Behaviour

The only room Joyce, Bob and Hopper don't need to destroy is the entrance room, so they can re-enter this one after exiting it. They should move one room east or south, eliminate its demodog and then re-enter the entrance room. From that point, there are eight options to complete the path. Here are the possible solutions:

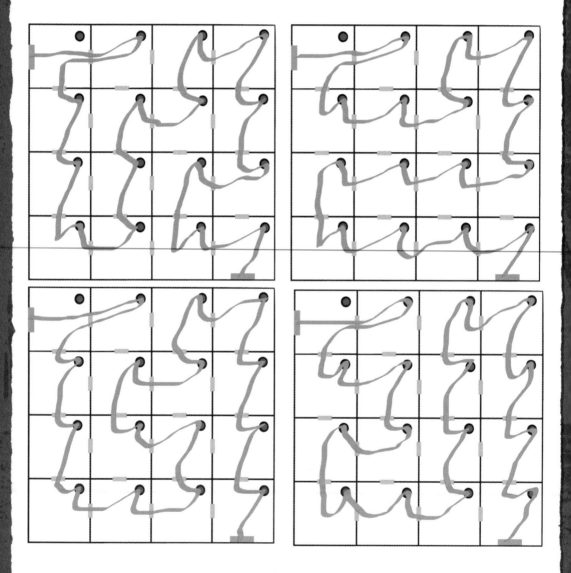

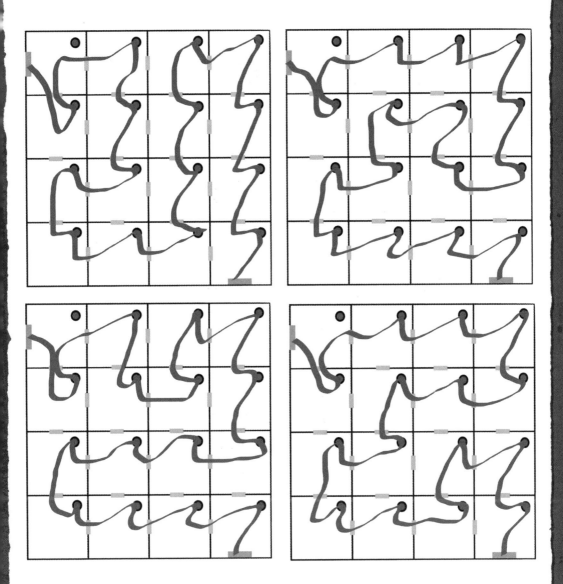

90 – Easy Peasy

There are 7,000 possible different codes that can't be cracked. As the code's first digit can't be 0, 5 or 7, there are 7 possible numbers it can be. All 10 digits can be used for the second, third and fourth numbers, however, so 7 x 10 x 10 x 10 = 7,000.

91 – Breaker Breaking

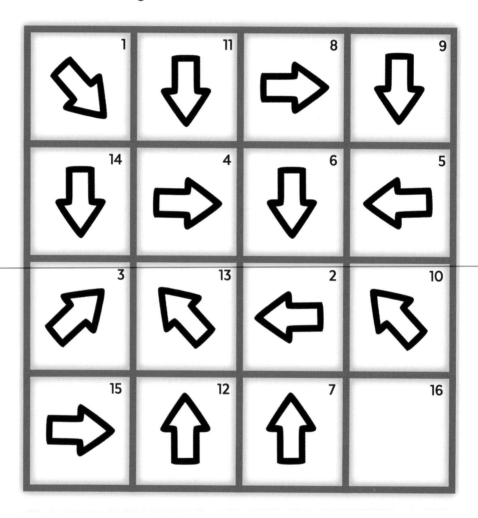

92 – Bob Newby, Superhero
Farewell.

93 – "Shirley"
The only days Axel can say that he lied on the previous day are Mondays and Thursdays, while the only days Mick can say she lied on the previous day are Thursdays and Sundays. Therefore, the only day they can both say that is Thursday, which must be the actual day.

94 – Dividing the Spoils, Spoiling the Divide
There were 79 Twinkies in the original pile. The next possible number that would have met the listed criteria would be 160, but that's larger than the given number of 50 - 100 Twinkies.

95 – An Eleven and an Eight
Axel has the Queen and Eight of Clubs, Mick has the Ace and Ten of Hearts, Dottie has the Jack and Seven of Spades, and Funshine has the King and Nine of Diamonds.

96 – Crime Does Pay, Very Slightly
The probability is 14.3 per cent. 22 per cent of the gas station owners are unarmed and 65 per cent don't have children. Therefore, 22 per cent x 65 per cent, or 14.3 per cent, of gas-station owners are unarmed and have no children.

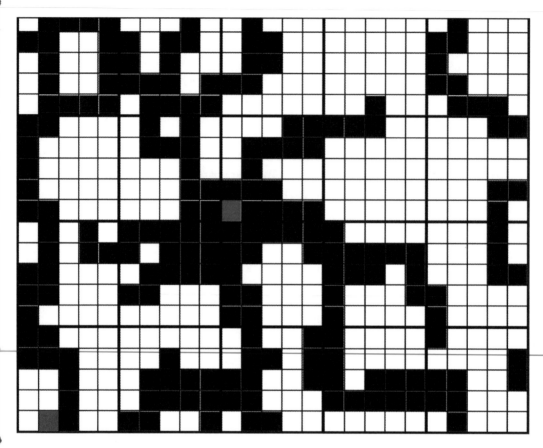

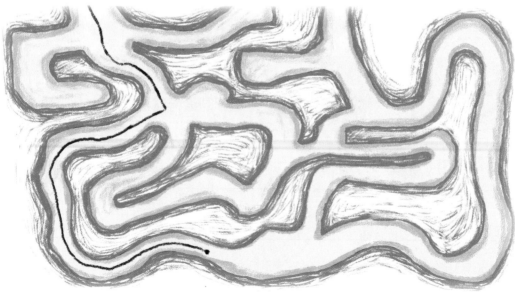

98 – "Drench It"

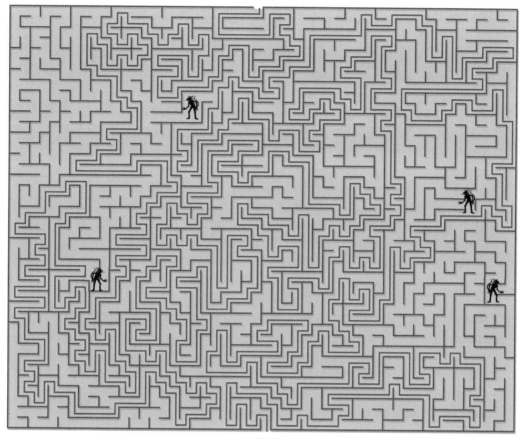

START

END

99 – Healing a Rift

$(2^6 - 1) / 2^6 = 63/64$

100 – The Kind of Town Where Nothing Ever Happens

"Justice."

PICTURE CREDITS

The publishers would like to thank the following sources for their kind permission to reproduce the pictures in this book.

Shutterstock: /32 pixels: 27R; /Babich Alexander: 35, 50-51; /alexblacksea: 114; /alexwhite: 52; /ALMAGAMI: 141BL; /Amili: 110BR; /aperturesound: 14BKG; /Chubykin Arkady: 97; /Andrey Arkusha: 144BR; /Mile Atansov: 141BR; /Black creator: 98B; /Jacob Boomsma: 68-69; /Steve Bramall: 36, 73; /Pra Chid: 8, 116; /Country Gate Productions: 17; /crwpitman: 80-81; /Chepko Danil Vitalevich: 134, 135; /Oliver Denker: 78-79; /Claudio Divizia: 24BL; /Double Brain: 43; /emka74: 14BR; /endeavor: 25; /Melinda Fawver: 100BL; /Sheila Fitzgerald: 99BR; /R. Formidable: 102; /Vladimir Gjorgiev: 32; /GoodStudio: 120; /gst: 10, 104; /Heimhard: 130BR; /Brent Hofacker: 130BL; /Keith Homan: 99BL, 99BC, ; /inxti: 59; /Ksenia Ivashkevich: 75; /jeabsam: 60; /JoeyPhoto: 58; /Kaesler Media: 5, 14C; /Harry Kasyanov: 128; /koyash07: 41; /Petr Lerch: 40; /Martin Lisner: 77; /Louella938: 118; /Jacob Lund: 146; /Marbury: 21; /Kateryna Mashkevych: 39; /mayu85: 42BR; /Phil McDonald: 95; /Mega Pixel: 84; /Mihalex: 70; /MoreVector: 37; /Artem Musaev: 49; /Dmitry Natashin: 147BKG; /Kelly Nelson: 111; /Orla: 26BL; /Rina Oshi: 110BL; /PanicAttack: 147BC; /Ioannis Pantzi: 31; /Giannis Papanikos: 27B; /Pavel L Photo and Video: 129; /Olga Popova: 23; /Maisei Raman: 131; /Ranjith Ravindran: 98BKG; /Yevhen Rehulian: 34; /RestonImages: 4, 15; /Romrodphoto: 88-89; /Michael Schymkiw: 90-91; /Arporn Seemaroj: 127; /sergign: 94; /Yurchanka Siarhei: 153BR; /simplegraphic: 18; /skopva: 24BR; /Ljupco Smokovski: 100BR; /Studio Barcelona: 93; /Nowik Sylwia: 147BL; /Thumbelina: 30; /Tiger Images: 66; /Tkray: 126; /Vanzyst: 144BKG; /Vinicius Tupinamba: 44-45; /Volkova Vera: 62, 62-63BKG; /VladisChern: 48; /VORTEX: 122-123; /Winiki: 26BR; /Slobodan Zivkovic: 76

Every effort has been made to acknowledge correctly and contact the source and/or copyright holder of each picture and Carlton Books Limited apologises for any unintentional errors or omissions that will be corrected in future editions of this book.